# EPHES

## The Church: God's Servant

We are God's workmanship,
created in Christ Jesus to do good works,
which God prepared in advance for us to do.
*Ephesians 2:10*

Prepared from Materials Provided by Walter L. Rosin
Edited by James H. Heine

CPH.
SAINT LOUIS

Series editors: Thomas J. Doyle and Rodney L. Rathmann

Assistant to the editors: Cindi Anderson

We solicit your comments and suggestions concerning this material. Please write to Product Manager, Adult Bible Studies, Concordia Publishing House, 3558 S. Jefferson Avenue, St. Louis, MO 63118-3968.

The introduction, "Ephesians: What's It All About?" is adapted from the introduction to the Captivity Letters and the introduction to Ephesians by Martin H. Franzmann in the *Concordia Self-Study Commentary*, copyright © 1971, 1979 by Concordia Publishing House. All rights reserved.

Quotations from the Small Catechism are from *Luther's Small Catechism*, 1986 translation. Copyright © 1986 by Concordia Publishing House. All rights reserved.

Copyright © 1977, 1996 Concordia Publishing House
3558 South Jefferson Avenue, St. Louis, MO 63118-3968
Manufactured in the United States of America

1   2   3   4   5   6   7   8   9   10          05   04   03   02   01   00   99   98   97   96

# Contents

**Introduction**—Ephesians: What's It All About?                    5

**Lesson 1**—A Letter from a Friend                                 7

**Lesson 2**—Chosen!                                               13

**Lesson 3**—Created!                                              18

**Lesson 4**—Transferred!                                          23

**Lesson 5**—Primed for Prayer and Praise                          28

**Lesson 6**—Guaranteed!                                           33

**Lesson 7**—Revealed!                                             38

**Lesson 8**—United!                                               42

**Lesson 9**—Blessed!                                              47

**Lesson 10**—Committed!                                           53

**Lesson 11**—Related!                                             58

**Lesson 12**—Employed!                                            64

**Lesson 13**—Armed!                                               68

**Leaders Notes**
Preparing to Teach Ephesians                                       77

**Lesson   1**                                                     81

**Lesson   2**                                                     84

**Lesson   3**                                                     86

**Lesson  4**                                                                88

**Lesson  5**                                                                90

**Lesson  6**                                                                92

**Lesson  7**                                                                94

**Lesson  8**                                                                97

**Lesson  9**                                                               100

**Lesson 10**                                                               103

**Lesson 11**                                                               105

**Lesson 12**                                                               109

**Lesson 13**                                                               112

# Introduction

# Ephesians
# What's It All About?

Ephesians is one of the four Captivity Letters of the apostle Paul. Along with Philippians, Colossians, and Philemon, Paul wrote his letter to the Ephesians while he was a prisoner of Roman authorities.

Church tradition ascribes these letters to Paul's first imprisonment in Rome (A.D. 59–61). This incarceration in the capital of the Empire followed Paul's final trip to Jerusalem (Acts 21–23) and his two-year internment in Caesarea (Acts 24:27).

Luke in his Acts of the Apostles tells the moving story of how Paul journeyed to Jerusalem bearing gifts from the Gentile churches to the church at Jerusalem. He recounts how Paul was arrested after a riot erupted in the temple courts, how he was sent to Caesarea for his own safety, where he languished in prison for two years at the whim of Felix, and how, finally, he was sent to Rome by Festus to appear before Caesar (Nero), where for another "two whole years Paul stayed there in his own rented house and welcomed all who came to see him" (Acts 28:30).

In spite of the hardship and uncertainty, Paul was not idled by the chains that enshackled him. Luke tells us this about Paul's stay in Rome: "Boldly and without hindrance he preached the kingdom of God and taught about the Lord Jesus Christ" (Acts 28:31).

Paul himself links his letter to the Ephesians to his letters to the Colossians and to Philemon. Tychicus is the bearer of the letter to the Ephesians (6:21). He is also the bearer of the letter to the Colossians, and the slave Onesimus is returning to Colossae with him (Col. 4:7–9).

We can infer one of Paul's motives for sending his letter to the Ephesians from a statement made by Paul near the end of the letter, "Pray also for me" (6:19). Paul's situation provided another motive. He was "an ambassador in chains" (6:20). Though his chains denied him the joy of "strengthening the churches" (Acts 15:41) in person, he could encourage and build up the faith of the Ephesians by means of pen and paper.

The message of Paul's letter to the Ephesians is an important one. It's all about the church—and it's all about us. In one sense Paul's letter was a message written to a particular group of people (the young church at Ephesus in Asia Minor—modern-day Turkey) at a particular time. In another sense Paul's letter to his Ephesian friends is a message for the whole church of all time. In that sense it is a message for us. It is *God's* message for us in the time and place in which we live: "We are God's workmanship, created in Christ Jesus to do good works, which God prepared in advance for us to do" **(Ephesians 2:10).**

# Lesson 1

# A Letter from a Friend

## Theme Verse

We are God's workmanship, created in Christ Jesus to do good works, which God prepared in advance for us to do. **Ephesians 2:10**

## Goal

In this first session we will learn about the historical setting of Paul's letter to the Ephesians, discover the theme of his letter, and gain an overview of the entire epistle.

## What's Going On Here?

Whenever you receive an important message, it's a good idea to summarize the message—to try to capture the idea of the message in a single phrase. Fortunately, we have such a one-phrase summary of Ephesians. We find it in chapter 2, verse 10.

Read **Ephesians 2:10** (printed above as our theme verse); then paraphrase the verse in your own words. What does this verse say about God's action? About our response to God's action?

## Searching the Scriptures

Another task of those who want to understand a message is to determine the facts surrounding that message. When a newspaper reporter writes about an event, he or she will seek to answer five questions: *who, what, when, where,* and *why.* We've already summarized *what* the message of Ephesians is. Now we need to answer the questions *who*, *when*, *where*, and *why*.

# Who

In **1:1** the writer of the letter is identified as Paul. In **6:21** the bearer of the letter is identified as Tychicus. But to whom was the letter written? Who are the *we* referred to in **2:10**?

Most translations of the Bible include the words *in Ephesus* in **1:1**; yet others do not. The reason for this is both simple and complex: While church tradition has always named the Ephesians as the recipients of this letter, and while many ancient copies of Paul's letter include *in Ephesus* in verse 1, the most ancient manuscripts we have today do not.

Because the earliest copies of Paul's letter do not contain the words *in Ephesus*, some Bible scholars and translators believe that Ephesians is a general letter to Christian congregations in the area where Ephesus was the largest and most important city. If this letter was written to be read in a number of churches, perhaps we could even insert the name of our own congregation in the greeting in **1:1**. This letter is a message also to *us*.

1. Colossians is a letter very much like Ephesians. Read **Colossians 4:7, 16.** How do these two verses support the idea of letters being circulated?

2. Read **Revelation 1:11.** To what congregations might this letter have been circulated?

3. Locate Ephesus on a map. Also find on the map the location of some of the congregations near Ephesus.

# When

We cannot determine exactly when this letter was written, but we do know that it was written sometime after the Christian congregations in and around Ephesus were formed.

1. Read **Acts 18:18–28.** Among whom were the first to bring the Gospel to Ephesus?

2. Paul returned to Ephesus on his third missionary journey. Read **Acts 19:1–10.** Describe Paul's ministry in Ephesus. For how long did he do this?

While the date for the writing of this letter is uncertain, it likely occurred after Paul's third missionary journey (A.D. 53–57). If, as many scholars think, Ephesians was written during Paul's first Roman imprisonment (see the introduction and below), it would have been written between 59 and 61.

## Where

In answering the who and when questions, we have already partially answered the question *where.* We now know in general where the recipients of the letter were located. But from where was this letter written?

As we noted in the introduction, church tradition ascribes Rome as Paul's residence when he composed this letter, and many modern-day Bible scholars believe that church tradition accurately reflects Paul's location and circumstances. Yet some Bible scholars believe Paul wrote Ephesians during his two-year imprisonment in Caesarea, while others speculate that Paul may have composed Ephesians while he was in jail in Ephesus itself.

While Paul himself does not name the city from which he wrote Ephesians, we can tell something about his personal situation. What information can we glean from **Ephesians 3:1, 13; 4:1; and 6:18–20?**

# Why

Often we write letters simply to share our thoughts with friends, especially when there is no chance that we will see them soon. That may be true of this letter from Paul. He may have simply wanted to share his thoughts about what the church is and what it should mean in the lives of the readers.

1. Paul's farewell address to the elders of the congregation at Ephesus is recorded in **Acts 20:17–38.** Read the first part of that farewell address in **verses 17–25.** Why would it have been important to Paul to share his thoughts with the congregation at Ephesus?

2. Now read **verses 26–38.** What warning does Paul have for the leaders of the Ephesian congregation?

3. What encouragement does he give?

# The Word for Us

Ephesus was a great center of trade, commerce, and industry, a crossroads of east and west. It was fertile ground for the work of Paul and for the work of the Ephesian church. Yet it was dangerous ground, too, for Paul warns his Ephesian friends of "savage wolves," who will come and who "will not spare the flock" **(Acts 20:29).**

1. With what kind of "wolves" does the church contend today?

2. What kind of challenges do we, as Christians, face in today's world?

3. What kind of challenges does your congregation face?

4. Paul also had a word of comfort for his Ephesian friends at their parting. What comfort can we gain from Paul's words in **Acts 20:32,** even when we are confronted by "wolves."

5. As God's servants "created in Christ Jesus to do good works" **(Ephesians 2:10),** we have many opportunities to share God's blessings. List five ways you can share God's blessings in your community this week. Add to the list if you so choose.

# To Do This Week

Now that we have found out some information about the message to us in Ephesians, we are ready to read the message itself.

*Read the entire letter this week. Use the following symbols to help prepare you for further discussion:*

* for a passage or section that is especially meaningful or which gave you a new insight
? for something that you do not understand or about which you would like more information
↓ for a promise from God or a command for your life
→ for a direction for your relationship with others
↑ for a response to God for His blessings

Before you begin reading, pray for the Holy Spirit's guidance.

# Closing

Sing or speak together the words of "O Word of God Incarnate."

O Word of God incarnate,
O Wisdom from on high,
O Truth unchanged, unchanging,
O Light of our dark sky:
We praise You for the radiance
That from the hallowed page,
A lantern to our footsteps,
Shines on from age to age.

The Church from You, dear Master,
Received the gift divine;
And still that light is lifted
O'er all the earth to shine.
It is the chart and compass
That, all life's voyage through,
Mid mists and rocks and quicksands
Still guides, O Christ, to You.

Oh, make Your Church, dear Savior,
A lamp of burnished gold
To bear before the nations
Your true light as of old!
Oh, teach Your wand'ring pilgrims
By this their path to trace
Till, clouds and darkness ended,
They see You face to face!

# Lesson 2

# Chosen!

## Theme Verses

Praise be to the God and Father of our Lord Jesus Christ, who has blessed us in the heavenly realms with every spiritual blessing in Christ. For He chose us in Him before the creation of the world to be holy and blameless in His sight. **Ephesians 1:3–4**

## Goal

In this session we will learn that all who belong to the church are members only because of God's choice by grace in Christ. As the Holy Spirit works through God's Word, we will be moved to thank God for His undeserved love.

## What's Going On Here?

Throughout our lives we are faced with choices—choices of cars, television sets, friends, schools, jobs. Almost everything in life involves a choice.

Think about the choices you make. Why do you make the choices you do?

## Searching the Scriptures

**Ephesians 1:3–4** tells about a choice God made. He chose us. Read those verses and take the following true-false quiz.

___ God chose us because we are beautiful people.

___ God chose us because of our superior intelligence.

___ God chose us because He had no other choice.

___ God chose us because we chose Him first.

___ God chose us because He knew we would believe in Him and accept Christ as our Savior.

___ God chose us because of His grace in Jesus Christ.

Now read **Ephesians 2:8–9** and look at your answers to the quiz. Would you change any of your answers now? Why or why not?

To be chosen means that there is something special involved. Usually in the choices we make that "something special" is in the person or object chosen. But the "something special" that caused God to choose us is quite different. That "something special" is His grace.

1. How do you define the word *grace?*

Paul's purpose is not to tell us *why* God chose us but simply to stress the fact *that* He chose us to be His own and that He chose us *in Christ.*

2. Read through **Ephesians 1:3–14.** How many times do the phrases "in Christ" and "in Him" and similar phrases appear?

3. Now look at **John 1:17.** What do the passages you have read tell you about God's grace?

# The Word for Us

Have you ever been a candidate for office—for a position you wanted but for which you weren't chosen? Or have you ever won an election to a position you really desired?

1. How do you feel when you are not chosen for something for which you desire?

2. How do you feel when you are chosen? How do you feel toward those who chose you?

3. Look at Paul's expression of praise and thanksgiving in **Ephesians 1:3–23.** List some of the words in that doxology that deserve special attention. Use one or more of these words to create your own expression of praise and thanks to God.

4. Look at **Ephesians 1:3–14** once again. In which words does Paul emphasize the work of the Father and the Holy Spirit in choosing us and saving us?

5. In his explanation to the Third Article of the Apostles' Creed, Martin Luther, the great reformer of the church, expresses the same ideas about our salvation that Paul expresses in **Ephesians 1:3–14:**

> I believe that I cannot by my own reason or strength believe in Jesus Christ, my Lord, or come to Him; but the Holy Spirit has called me by the Gospel, enlightened me with His gifts, sanctified and kept me in true faith.
>
> In the same way He calls, gathers, enlightens, and sanctifies the whole Christian church on earth, and keeps it with Jesus Christ in the one true faith.
>
> In this Christian church He daily and richly forgives all my sins and the sins of all believers.
>
> On the Last Day He will raise me and all the dead, and give eternal life to me and all believers in Christ.
>
> This is most certainly true.

What comfort can we gain from confessing that we are in Christ?

# Closing

Have participants who are willing share their expressions of praise and thanks to God from the activity in "The Word for Us." Or speak or sing together the words of "Amazing Grace! How Sweet the Sound."

> Amazing grace! How sweet the sound
> That saved a wretch like me!
> I once was lost but now am found,
> Was blind but now I see!
>
> The Lord has promised good to me,
> His word my hope secures;
> He will my shield and portion be
> As long as life endures.

Through many dangers, toils, and snares
I have already come;
His grace has brought me safe so far,
His grace will see me home.

Yes, when this flesh and heart shall fail
And mortal life shall cease,
Amazing grace shall then prevail
In heaven's joy and peace.

# Lesson 3

# Created!

## Theme Verse

For we are God's workmanship, created in Christ Jesus to do good works, which God prepared in advance for us to do. **Ephesians 2:10**

## Goal

In this session we will seek to understand and appreciate that our new life in Christ is the result of the workmanship of God, who alone can change our human condition from death to life.

## What's Going On Here?

St. Paul says, "We are [His] workmanship, *created* in Christ Jesus" (**2:10**, italics added). That word *created* is a powerful verb. In our everyday speech we use it loosely to speak of the artist who "creates" a masterpiece, the chef who "creates" a gourmet meal, the composer who "creates" an opera, and the peace-disturber who "creates" a riot.

The Bible, however, is much more selective in the use of the term. It is so selective, in fact, that it never speaks of anyone creating except God. And it rarely uses the term to describe the bringing into being of a new thing out of already existing items. The verb "to create" is used in the Bible to express the idea of God bringing something into being out of nothing.

## Searching the Scriptures

Look up the following passages:
- **Genesis 1:1, 3**
- **Psalm 51:10**
- **Psalm 104:30**
- **Isaiah 43:15**

- **2 Corinthians 5:17–18**
- **Colossians 1:15–16**

1. What do these passages tell you about the who, what, and how of creation?

2. What does this tell you about your creation "in Christ Jesus" spoken of by Paul in **Ephesians 2:10?**

We have seen that to be "created" means to be brought into existence out of nothing by God. But are we really nothing? Is that what Paul is implying when he says we are "created in Christ Jesus"?

3. **Ephesians 2:1–3** is a blanket statement that describes all of us. Read these verses. What does Paul say here about the human condition?

4. What does Paul mean by the "cravings of our sinful nature" and "its desires and thoughts"? You may wish to read **Romans 1:18–32,** where Paul goes into greater detail about these concepts. Other passages to check are **Colossians 2:8; 1 Timothy 6:3–10; Jude 16;** and **Galatians 5:19–21.**

5. Now look at the phrases below, most of which you have probably heard or seen. To what do these phrases appeal? Is it wrong to use them?
- "Alive with pleasure"
- "For the man/woman who has everything"
- "Clothes make the man"

The Scriptures clearly point to the fact that anyone who is controlled by the "cravings of our sinful nature" and "its desires and thoughts" is dead **(2:1)**. And to be dead is to be nothing. That's what everyone is apart from Christ.

# The Word for Us

We were nothing, dead in our "transgressions and sins" **(2:1)**. But "God ... made us alive with Christ" **(2:4–5)**. From the point of our being nothing, God has brought a whole new being into existence. We are *His* workmanship **(2:10)**. He has created us "in Christ." We are *His* new creation. He has brought us out of death to fullness of life in His Son.

1. Read carefully **Ephesians 2:4–10.** What moved God to create us as His new beings?

2. According to **John 3:16–17,** how did God accomplish this?

3. Our Baptism has a lot to do with our creation as God's new beings. Read **Romans 6:3–4.** How does your Baptism into the death and resurrec-

tion of Christ relate to your being brought by God from death to life?

To aid your discussion, consider Martin Luther's answers to the questions "What benefits does Baptism give?" and "What does such baptizing with water indicate?"

> [Baptism] works forgiveness of sins, rescues from death and the devil, and gives eternal salvation to all who believe this, as the words and promises of God declare.

> It indicates that the Old Adam in us should by daily contrition and repentance be drowned and die with all sins and evil desires, and that a new man should daily emerge and arise to live before God in righteousness and purity forever.

# Closing

Sing or speak together the words of "Baptized into Your Name Most Holy."

> Baptized into Your name most holy,
> O Father, Son, and Holy Ghost,
> I claim a place, though weak and lowly,
> Among Your seed, Your chosen host.
> Buried with Christ and dead to sin,
> I have Your Spirit now within.
>
> My loving Father, here You take me
> Henceforth to be Your child and heir;
> My faithful Savior, here You make me
> The fruit of all Your sorrows share;
> O Holy Ghost, You comfort me
> Though threat'ning clouds around I see.
>
> O faithful God, You never fail me;
> Your cov'nant surely will abide.
> Let not eternal death assail me
> Should I transgress it on my side!
> Have mercy when I come defiled;
> Forgive, lift up, restore Your child.

All that I am and love most dearly,
Receive it all, O Lord, from me.
Oh, let me make my vows sincerely,
And help me Your own child to be!
Let nothing that I am or own
Serve any will but Yours alone.

# Lesson 4

# Transferred!

## Theme Verses

Because of His great love for us, God, who is rich in mercy, made us alive with Christ even when we were dead in transgressions—it is by grace you have been saved. **Ephesians 2:4–5**

## Goal

In this session we will seek to understand and appreciate that we have been transferred from the power of Satan to full citizenship in the kingdom of Christ. We will begin to discover ways in which we can exercise our privileges and responsibilities as citizens of His kingdom.

## What's Going On Here?

Imagine yourself in this situation. You are employed by a boss who is a tyrant. No matter what you do, your boss is critical of your performance. "Can't you ever do anything right?" is his constant question that follows any task you perform.

You are so unhappy that you would like to change jobs. But you are an alien—a person who is in this country on a work permit—and unless you keep your present job, you are in danger of being deported. So you continue to work for your present boss, motivated solely by fear.

Then one day you discover that you have been transferred to another department. Suddenly your life changes. Your new boss is kind and loving toward you. He goes out of his way to praise you when you do a job well. Even when you make mistakes, he quietly corrects your errors and never mentions them to you, except to point out at times where you went wrong and how you might avoid making the same mistakes in the future. After a few months he even helps you obtain your citizenship papers and pays all the necessary fees to register you as a citizen.

Now all your old fears are gone. Your life is changed completely. Now your work is motivated not by fear but by love and gratitude toward your new boss who has given you a new and happy life.

## Searching the Scriptures

The story in the previous section is somewhat analogous to a situation each of us has experienced. Our old boss was Satan.

1. Examine **Ephesians 2:2** carefully. What does this passage tell you about Satan? Who is he?

2. What are some of his activities?

3. Now look at **Mark 4:15; Luke 13:10–17; John 13:26–27; Acts 5:1–4;** and **1 Corinthians 7:5.** What do you think Paul means by his reference to "the ruler of the kingdom of the air"?

4. How does Satan hold his power over people? **Hebrews 2:14–15** will give you the answer.

## The Word for Us

Because of Jesus' once-for-all sacrifice, we are no longer under the power of the tyrant Satan. We have been transferred! Transferred from the power of Satan to the care of the King. We are members of the kingdom of

Christ—solely by His grace! Paul reminds us that God has "raised us up with Christ and seated us with Him in the heavenly realms" **(Ephesians 2:6).** No one needs a rocket to get into the "heavenly realms." All that is needed is that which God has given—faith in Christ.

1. Read **Ephesians 2:6–10.** What is the result of our having been transferred into the kingdom of Christ?

2. How do you respond to that which God has done for us in Christ Jesus? See **Ephesians 2:10.**

3. Paul describes his readers as having been "foreigners and aliens" **(2:11–12, 19).** What were the causes of that alienation? What was the result of that alienation? Search **Ephesians 2:11–13** to find your answers.

The transfer is complete! Those who were foreigners are now citizens with all the privileges and responsibilities that citizenship brings.

That transfer was not our doing. We did not choose to become citizens of Christ's kingdom. He chose us and paid the price required to make us fully accredited citizens in His kingdom.

4. What price did Christ pay to make us citizens of His kingdom? **(2:13–16)?**

5. What are our privileges and responsibilities as citizens (**2:19–22**)?

6. What are some ways in which we can exercise our privileges and responsibilities?

God has transferred us—from the tyranny of Satan to His care as King, from being aliens to full citizenship in Christ's kingdom. All this is God's doing, not ours. For all this we can only, as Luther says in his explanation to the First Article of the Apostles' Creed, "thank and praise, serve and obey Him."

7. How might you thank, praise, serve, and obey Jesus Christ?

# Closing

Sing or speak together the words of "I Love Your Kingdom, Lord."

I love Your kingdom, Lord,
The place of Your abode;
The Church our blest Redeemer saved
With His own precious blood.

I love Your Church, O God!
Its walls before You stand,
Dear as the apple of Your eye
And graven on Your hand.

Beyond my highest joy
I prize its heav'nly ways,
Its sweet communion, solemn vows,
Its hymns of love and praise.

Sure as Your truth shall last,
To Zion shall be giv'n
The brightest glories earth can yield
And brighter bliss of heav'n.

# Lesson 5

# Primed for Prayer and Praise

## Theme Verses

In Him we have redemption through His blood, the forgiveness of sins, in accordance with the riches of God's grace that He lavished on us with all wisdom and understanding. **Ephesians 1:7–8**

## Goal

In this session we will seek to express the joy and gratitude that we experience as people who have received forgiveness of sins and eternal life by God's lavish grace through faith in Jesus Christ.

## What's Going On Here?

Holidays are important days for us. They provide a break in our day-to-day routine. Over the past few decades, however, the meaning and purpose of many of our holidays has changed. With the changing of the day of our celebration from the actual day on which a holiday falls to the Monday closest to that day, many holidays have become nothing more than an opportunity for us to enjoy a three-day weekend.

This is a far cry from the original intent of those who set aside these holidays. They were set aside as days on which to remember a man or an event that is important in the history of our country or of our world. Activities on that day would then recall that person or event, express our appreciation for that portion of our history, and encourage us to draw inspiration and encouragement from the person or event being remembered. Thus the celebration of such a holiday focused our attention on the purpose for the celebration.

Understanding that original purpose for celebrating holidays will help bring us closer to an understanding of that which Paul celebrates in certain sections of his letter to the Ephesians. In these sections, Paul remembers past events, praises God, expresses appreciation, and prays that his readers will draw inspiration and encouragement from what God has done for them and in them.

Paul's celebration, however, is not limited to a certain day. It is an ongoing celebration that pervades his life. Whenever he remembers what God has done, he is moved to break out in words of praise and thanksgiving. That is how it is in the life of the Christian. We are primed for prayer and praise by the wonderful works that God has done in the world—and in us!

## Searching the Scriptures

Paul's words of celebration are the result of his remembrance of what had happened in his own life and in the lives of his readers. He remembered that he who once been a persecutor of Christians had been changed by the Spirit of God into an apostle of Jesus Christ. And because he had been changed by the Spirit of God, transferred into the kingdom of Christ, he could not help remembering that it was the grace of God that had brought that change about.

### Remember

Paul's words of celebration were also occasioned by other remembrances. Paul tells of some of the remembrances that moved him to celebration in **1:4; 1:7; 1:13;** and **1:20.**

1. List these remembrances of Paul.

2. Look back on your own life. What are some remembrances of things that God has done in your life that move you to celebrate?

# Praise

There are many ways to celebrate what God has done. Paul gives a good example. Whenever he remembers what God has done, his words of praise almost tumble over one another.

1. Look at Paul's words of praise in **1:3** and **3:20–21.** What words would you use to express similar praise to God today?

2. Where and when might you use these words? What might move you to speak such words of praise to God?

# Thanks

Not only does Paul praise God, but he also thanks God. Note that in **1:15–16,** it is *people* for whom Paul thanks God—people who have been chosen by God, changed by Him, and transferred into Christ's kingdom.

Paul's words of thanksgiving encourage us to thank God for people who have been important in sharing their faith and in so doing in nourishing and sustaining our Christian life. Take a moment now and make a list of people for whom you wish to thank God.

# Pray

In his words of celebration, Paul remembered that our future is as dependent on God as our past was due to His love and grace. Therefore Paul had some things for which he was asking also.

Look at **Ephesians 1:16–19a** and **3:14–19.** Notice that the requests that Paul makes are more for others than for himself. What does this say to you about your prayers?

# The Word for Us

One writer, commenting on **Ephesians 1:15,** wrote that "much of the tension within and without the Church springs from cold justice severed from the warmth of love." In another place he says, "The lack of awareness that there is a connection between the various local congregations has too often promoted the schismatic spirit as 'Lone Ranger' preachers have led congregations in self-centered service."

1. Do you agree with these statements? If such a situation should arise in your own church or community, how could you seek to reunite justice and love?

2. What can we include in our daily prayers in order to ask God to help us be less self-centered and self-serving in our concerns?

# To Do This Week

In Paul's words of celebration he remembered what God had done, praised and thanked God, and prayed for God's blessings in the future.

As part of your devotional life this week, plan your own celebration in which you remember what God has done in your life, speak or sing words of praise to Him, thank Him for people who have been important in nourishing and sustaining your faith-life, and pray for God's blessings for yourself and for others.

# Closing

Speak or sing together the words of "When All Your Mercies, O My God."

When all Your mercies, O my God,
My waking soul surveys,
Transported with the view, I'm lost
In wonder, love, and praise.

Ten thousand thousand precious gifts
My daily thanks employ;
Nor is the least a cheerful heart
That tastes those gifts with joy.

Through ev'ry passing phase of life
Your goodness I'll pursue
And after death, in distant worlds,
The glorious theme renew.

Through all eternity to You
A joyful song I'll raise;
But, oh, eternity's too short
To utter all Your praise!

# Lesson 6

# Guaranteed!

## Theme Verses

In Him you also, who have heard the word of truth, the gospel of your salvation, and have believed in Him, were sealed with the promised Holy Spirit, which is the guarantee of our inheritance until we acquire possession of it, to the praise of His glory. **Ephesians 1:13–14 RSV**

## Goal

In this session, by the power of the Holy Spirit working through God's Word, we will strengthen the firm conviction that our eternal destiny is life with Christ forever.

## What's Going On Here?

Whenever you make a major purchase such as a car, a furnace, or a stove, you usually get a warranty. This represents an agreement by the manufacturer that if anything goes wrong with the item you have purchased within a certain period of time, it will be repaired or replaced free of charge, subject to certain restrictions listed in the warranty.

The warranty—guarantee—is designed to assure you that the item you have purchased is free from defects in material or workmanship and will function as it should. Sometimes, however, this doesn't really mean much, for when you read the fine print you discover that the manufacturer's agreement is often limited to certain parts, may not include labor, and is for a short period of time. So it often happens that a breakdown occurs either in the parts not under warranty or just after the time period covered has expired. Therefore, when you purchase an item under warranty, it's a good idea to read the agreement carefully to be sure you understand its terms.

If it is important to understand the terms of a product warranty, how much more important it is when you stake your whole life now and forever on a person or belief to ask the following: What guarantee do I have? What assurance is there that I am on the right track? How can I know for certain that what has been promised will actually come to pass?

## Searching the Scriptures

1. Paul was very sure of the person and belief on which he had staked his life. Examine a few of his statements to congregations in **Romans 8:31–38; 1 Thessalonians 5:23–24; Philippians 4:7** and to an individual in **2 Timothy 1:12**. Of what was Paul very sure?

Not all Christians are as sure as Paul about their eternal future. The story is told of a man who spent much of his time in the train station of a large city during the time when much travel was still being done by train. The man would approach a traveler about to board a train and ask, "Where are you going?" If the traveler responded by giving his or her destination, the man would reply, "That's not what I meant. Where are you going when you die?"

Here are some possible answers to the man's question:

- "I hope I go to heaven."
- "I think I will go to be with God."
- "God willing, I will go to heaven."
- "I don't know for sure, but I'm trying to live a good life so that I will go to heaven."

2. Do any of these phrases express your belief about your eternal future? If so, which one? If not, take a few moments now to write your responses to the question "Where are you going?"

3. Look closely at **Ephesians 1:11–14.** How could Paul be so sure of his eternal future?

4. What is our inheritance? How does the Holy Spirit guarantee our inheritance?

When the writers of Holy Scripture gave their testimony to what they believed, it was based on something that made them certain—so certain that they were willing to die for what they believed. There were many reasons for their certainty, but you could probably sum them all up in the word *God*. God's promises were not words alone, but they were words backed up by His mighty acts. It was to these mighty acts that the Holy Spirit kept pointing the biblical writers as the assurance of their eternal future.

5. Look up the following Bible passages and identify the mighty acts of God to which the Holy Spirit pointed Paul as the assurance of his eternal future:

**Romans 1:20**

**1 Corinthians 10:1–5**

**Acts 9**

**Acts 2:22–24**

6. Which of God's mighty acts do you think provided the surest guarantee for Paul?

# The Word for Us

1. What mighty acts of God assure you of your eternal future?

Ultimately, we can be sure of our eternal future because of the Holy Spirit. He is the guarantee.

2. Check **2 Corinthians 1:18–22** and **5:1–5.** How does the Holy Spirit guarantee our eternal future?

Through the Word and the Sacraments, the Holy Spirit works to create and to strengthen saving faith—to guarantee us that God's action in Jesus Christ applies to each one of us and that by God's grace we can be sure that we have life with Him forever. This is no limited warranty. The Holy Spirit is God's unconditional guarantee that we have an unlimited future with God.

# Closing

Sing or speak together the words of "O Holy Spirit, Enter In."

O Holy Spirit, enter in,
And in our hearts Your work begin,
And make our hearts Your dwelling.
Sun of the soul, O Light divine,
Around and in us brightly shine,
Your strength in us upwelling.
In Your radiance
Life from heaven
Now is given
Overflowing,
Gift of gifts beyond all knowing.

Left to ourselves, we surely stray;
Oh, lead us on the narrow way,
With wisest counsel guide us;
And give us steadfastness that we
May follow You forever free,
No matter who derides us.
Gently heal those
Hearts now broken;
Give some token
You are near us,
Whom we trust to light and cheer us.

O mighty Rock, O Source of life,
Let Your good Word in doubt and strife
Be in us strongly burning
That we be faithful unto death
And live in love and holy faith,
From You true wisdom learning.
Lord, Your mercy
On us shower;
By Your power
Christ confessing,
We will cherish all Your blessing.

# Lesson 7

# Revealed!

## Theme Verses

In reading this, then, you will be able to understand my insight into the mystery of Christ, which was not made known to men in other generations as it has now been revealed by the Spirit to God's holy apostles and prophets. **Ephesians 3:4–5**

## Goal

In this session we will seek to understand and appreciate the universal nature of God's plan of salvation revealed in His Word through the action of the Holy Spirit.

## What's Going On Here?

In a mystery story the plot is developed by the author, and therefore she alone knows the solution to the mystery, which is dramatically revealed to the reader only at the conclusion of the story. The author sees the whole plan and works it out in such a way as to maintain the interest of the reader. When the solution to the mystery is finally revealed, all the intricacies of the plot created by the author fall into place.

In **Ephesians 3:1–12,** St. Paul describes the actions of God for our salvation as a "mystery hidden for ages" (**3:9** RSV). Paul says that God's plan of salvation can be compared to a mystery story. God's plan was clear to Him from the very beginning, but if you didn't know the ending, you wouldn't understand the individual elements in the plan—the intricacies of the plot, so to speak. God's plan and purpose are not clear to us, therefore, unless we know the solution to the mystery. That solution is revealed to us by the Holy Spirit. Once we know that solution, however, we can understand all the intricacies of God's action.

# Searching the Scriptures

1. What are some of the parts of the mystery of God's plan? A brief overview of the Old Testament will give you some of them. Try making a list of events in the Old Testament that are part of the "mystery" of God's plan of salvation.

2. When you get to the New Testament, is God's plan of action clear right away? Look at **Acts 1:6–8; Matthew 10:5–6; 15:24; John 14:26; 16:12–13.** What do we learn from these verses?

3. Even Jesus' disciples did not at first understand the mystery of God's plan, even though Christ made some sweeping statements about the reason for His birth, life, death, and resurrection. Some of these statements are found in **John 3:14–17; Matthew 8:5–12; 21:33–41; 28:18–20.** What do these passages say about the purpose of Jesus' work on earth?

4. Why do you think Jesus' disciples failed to understand what Jesus was saying?

5. Now study **Ephesians 3:1–12.** What is the solution to the mystery?

6. How is the solution to the mystery revealed?

7. The events involved in the spreading of the Gospel as recorded in the book of Acts show how the solution to the mystery was revealed in the early history of the church. Read the accounts of some of these events in **Acts 8:26–39; 10:1–11:30; 13:1–4.** Who revealed the solution to the mystery?

8. What is that revelation?

# The Word for Us

God's mystery has been solved by His own action through the Holy Spirit. But do we really understand what God's revelation of the mystery means to us?

Are there ways in which we limit salvation to those of our own race, our own social class, our particular lifestyle? As you think about this, consider not only your words but also your actions and attitude. What sacrifices are you willing to make for foreign missions or for mission work among those who are different than you?

How do you feel about the following statements?

- *Mission work begins at home.*

- *The local congregation, if it is to be effective in its ministry, must choose to serve those it is best equipped to serve.*

- *Serving people of other ethnic backgrounds doesn't necessarily mean establishing personal contact with them. Most people feel more comfortable with people of their own ethnic group.*

Sometimes our attitudes and our actions speak louder than our words. We still need the Holy Spirit to remind us that salvation for *all* means just what it says. God sets no limits and neither can we!

# Closing

Close with the following prayer:

**Dear heavenly Father, we praise and thank You for the salvation won for us—and for all people—by the life, death, and resurrection of Your Son, Jesus Christ. Shine Your glorious light upon us, that we may walk in Your grace. Send Your Holy Spirit, that He may rule in our hearts. Bless Your church. Be with all who labor in Your name. Hear us for Jesus' sake. Amen.**

# Lesson 8

# United!

## Theme Verse

You are no longer foreigners and aliens, but fellow citizens with God's people and members of God's household. **Ephesians 2:19**

## Goal

In this session we will seek to realize and appreciate more fully the unity of the church that has been brought about by God's action in Christ.

## What's Going On Here?

If you were to ask someone today, "Do you belong to the church?" the response would probably be, "Which church?" When you think about the organizations in the world today that are called churches, the number of them is almost overwhelming. A new one seems to spring up almost every day.

The idea that the church is broken into individual competing segments is not new. It was there almost from the beginning, although the number of units was smaller at that time. But even though the church appears to be fragmented, it isn't really so. Led by the Spirit to write as he did, Paul took great pains to make that point clear. Read some of the things he has to say about the church in **Ephesians 1:22–23; 2:11–3:6;** and **4:1–6.**

## Searching the Scriptures

One of the words that plays a prominent role in Paul's message in **Ephesians 2:11–22** is *peace*. Notice, "[Christ] Himself is our peace. ... through the cross, by which He put to death their hostility" and "He came and preached peace." This could be summarized as "the Prince of peace, the price of peace, and the preaching of peace."

1. According to **Ephesians 2:11–22,** what two groups were enemies at the time Paul addressed his original readers?

2. What relationship does antagonism—separation—between God and people have to antagonism between people?

3. Do we have similar problems today? Give examples to back up your response.

Before Christ, the ceremonial law (including circumcision and food laws) separated Jews who kept it from Gentiles who did not. By His death, Christ destroyed the power of the Law to separate and to exclude. He died to reconcile both Jews and Gentiles to God, and in Him all believers are united. That is a favorite theme of Paul.

4. Christian churches usually don't have "commandments and regulations" **(2:15)** regarding things like circumcision and clean and unclean foods. But how do some churches establish new "commandments and regulations," thereby setting up a "dividing wall of hostility" **(2:14)?** Is there a need in your church for reconciliation and a greater peace?

The fact that peace has been made between God and people and between people through Christ needs to be made known. Christ made it known through His apostles and still makes it known through the Bible and His witnesses. The Spirit of Christ is active in our proclamations of the Good News of peace.

5. Read Christ's words to His disciples in **John 20:19–23.** What is the nature of Christ's peace?

6. Another prominent word used by Paul is *one.* Look at **Ephesians 2:14, 15, 16, 18** and **4:4–6.** How many times does the word *one* appear? Why do you suppose this is so important for Paul to proclaim?

7. Obviously, God wanted this concept stressed. On the basis of these verses would you say that the church is united or that the church should be united? Take some time to discuss especially the phrases in **4:4–6.**

As you read the first verses in **chapter 4,** it appears that there was a problem in the church which Paul was addressing, and that problem was a lack of unity—brought about by prejudice between Jew and Gentile. The point Paul seems to make is that all whom Christ has redeemed are part of the church. Prejudicial treatment or exclusion of some people because of the way they look or their ethnic background has no place in the church. The church is one. We seek to express that oneness. Why is this expression so important for people in the church? outside the church?

8. The basis for the unity of the church and for the expression of that unity is referred to in **Ephesians 2:19–22.** What does Paul mean when he says that the foundation of the church is "the apostles and prophets" and that the chief cornerstone is Christ?

9. Two pictures are used in **Ephesians 1:22–23** and **2:19–22** to describe the church. What are they?

10. If someone were looking to find Christ today, where would He be found?

# The Word for Us

1. Within the church there are no superior or inferior members. Look carefully at **Ephesians 3:6.** Why does Paul use three different phrases to describe the position of the Gentiles?

2. Do we ever give the impression that some are inferior members of the church? If so, who? How do we give that impression?

3. As a summary of what Paul is saying about the unity and equality of members of the church, read **1 Corinthians 12:12–27.** What does Paul say?

# Closing

Close by reading **1 Corinthians 12:12–27** in unison, or sing or speak the words of "The Church's One Foundation."

The Church's one foundation
Is Jesus Christ, her Lord;
She is His new creation
By water and the Word.
From heav'n He came and sought her
To be His holy bride;
With His own blood He bought her,
And for her life He died.

Elect from ev'ry nation,
Yet one o'er all the earth;
Her charter of salvation:
One Lord, one faith, one birth.
One holy name she blesses,
Partakes one holy food,
And to one hope she presses
With ev'ry grace endued.

Through toil and tribulation
And tumult of her war
She waits the consummation
Of peace forevermore
Till with the vision glorious
Her longing eyes are blest,
And the great Church victorious
Shall be the Church at rest.

Yet she on earth has union
With God, the Three in One,
And mystic sweet communion
With those whose rest is won.
O blessed heav'nly chorus!
Lord, save us by Your grace
That we, like saints before us,
May see You face to face.

# Lesson 9

# Blessed!

## Theme Verse

But to each one of us grace has been given as Christ apportioned it. **Ephesians 4:7**

## Goal

In this session we will seek to become more aware and appreciative of the gifts with which Christ has blessed the church and recognize that as individual gifts are used for the church, God's purposes will be achieved.

## What's Going On Here?

There are a number of things a parent can do for a child. Care can be provided, gifts can be given, support can be offered, direction can be established. Most of us had these things done for us when we were children, and those of us who have children of our own have probably tried to do them for our children also.

As a good parent provides for his or her child, so God provides for His church. He has blessed the church He created with everything it needs for life and growth. These blessings are described in **Ephesians 4:7–16.** We will talk about these blessings today.

## Searching the Scriptures

Read **Ephesians 4:7–16.**

Everyone in the church has been given gifts by God. The primary gift that each has been given is the gift of God's grace **(4:7).** That takes us right back to the thought expressed by Paul in **2:8–10.** Our membership in the church is solely by God's grace.

But not only is our membership in the church solely by God's grace, but whatever gifts we have for service in the church are also gifts of His grace. Christ gave them to His people when He ascended into heaven in order that they might carry on His work **(4:8).** We have no reason therefore to be proud of the gifts we have. They have been given to us, undeserved, purely out of God's grace.

1. What are the gifts of God mentioned in **Ephesians 4:11?**

2. Check **1 Corinthians 12:27–28** and **Romans 12:3–8.** What other gifts of God to the church are mentioned in these passages?

3. Obviously, Paul's lists are not meant to be all-inclusive. What other gifts of God to the church can you think of among members of your congregation? among members of the whole church? Remember, these gifts may range from artistic talent to administrative ability to agricultural knowledge or mechanical aptitude. List some of these gifts.

You may have noticed that God's gifts to the church are not just talents or characteristics. God's gifts to the church are primarily *people.* In Paul's list of gifts, he pays special attention to the *functions* the people who are God's gifts to the church are equipped to carry out. Once again, his list is not all-inclusive. The Scriptures point to other functions of the people of the church in such passages as **Acts 6:1–6; 1 Timothy 3:8; Titus 1:5;** and **Romans 16:1.**

4. What are some of the functions mentioned in these passages?

5. Now look again at the list you made in number 3. See whether you can differentiate among the functions of those listed.

# The Word for Us

The ascended Christ never gives gifts just to be giving them. They are always given for a purpose. This is true also of the gifts He gives to those who function as leaders in the church. They are given gifts not that they may attain position or power but in order to serve others. In fact, Christ gives gifts to all members of His body, the church, to use in service to Him. Paul says that leaders are given gifts "to prepare God's people for works of service, so that the body of Christ may be built up" **(Ephesians 4:12).**

1. What kind of "[preparing] God's people" is necessary to help members of your congregation use their gifts to carry out their tasks, their "works of service"?

2. What are some of those tasks? How do these tasks help your congregation to carry out its primary task **(Matthew 28:19–20)?**

3. Think of the tasks in which your congregation is involved and of the tasks in which individual members are involved as they use their gifts in service to Christ and His church. What role do the leaders of the congregation play in equipping people to carry out these tasks?

Leaders are to build up the body of Christ. That building includes both internal and external growth. Not only are the leaders of the church to seek to increase its numbers, but they are also to strengthen the members of the church.

4. What can church leaders do to "[build] up the body of Christ" (**Ephesians 2:12** RSV) in your congregation?

in your church body?

in the world?

Reread **Ephesians 4:11–16.** All these gifts and functions have a purpose. In fact, Paul gives a threefold purpose: unity of faith and knowledge of the Son of God, Christian maturity, and certainty of faith.

5. How does a lack of knowledge of the Son of God limit the unity of faith?

6. What are some of the marks of Christian maturity?

One of the purposes of God's gifts that St. Paul states is certainty of faith **(4:14).** We are aware that, as always, there are many different philosophies making a claim on the lives of people. Consider, for example, the influence today of various Eastern religious movements or of the New Age movement or of secular humanism or even of the allure of modern materialism.

7. How do we deal with anyone who makes counterclaims to the Christian faith?

8. What is the "truth" we are to speak? How do we speak that truth "in love"?

False claims cannot be ignored. They must be rejected. But while we must reject these false claims, we cannot reject the people who hold them. We must always remember that Christ died for them too.

# Closing

Sing or speak together the words from "Lord Jesus Christ, We Humbly Pray."

Lord Jesus Christ, we humbly pray
That we may feast on You today;
Beneath these forms of bread and wine
Enrich us with Your grace divine.

Give us, who share this wondrous food,
Your body broken and Your blood,
The grateful peace of sins forgiv'n,
The certain joys of heirs of heav'n.

By faith Your Word has made us bold
To seize the gift of love retold;
All that You are we here receive,
And all we are to You we give.

One bread, one cup, one body, we,
Rejoicing in our unity,
Proclaim Your love until You come
To bring Your scattered loved ones home.

Lord Jesus Christ, we humbly pray:
Oh, keep us steadfast till that day
When each will be Your welcomed guest
In heaven's high and holy feast.

# Lesson 10

# Committed!

## Theme Verses

Be imitators of God … and live a life of love. **Ephesians 5:1–2**

## Goal

In this session we will seek to increase our awareness that Christian faith involves commitment to a new way of life that reflects that faith. We will also seek to live that life as we are empowered by the Holy Spirit working through the Word of God.

## What's Going On Here?

Some people have the view that Christianity is only for the weak, for those unable to cope with the problems of life. Such a view of Christianity sees no real commitment on the part of those who claim to be Christians.

Nothing could be farther from the truth. The Bible makes this very clear. Consider, for example, the words of Christ in **Matthew 12:30; Luke 9:57–62;** and **Luke 14:15–33** or the words of warning to the church at Laodicea in **Revelation 3:14–16,** which are probably some of the harshest words ever written to any congregation.

Christian commitment is a necessary reflection of Christian faith, and such Christian commitment involves concern for others. No one is a member of the church by himself or herself. By virtue of Baptism and incorporation into the body of Christ through God's creating act, every Christian is involved with a concern for the whole world but especially for every other member of the body of Christ. With words such as "I tell you this, and insist on it in the Lord"; "you must no longer"; "must not be even a hint"; and "for of this you can be sure" **(Ephesians 4:17; 5:3, 5),** Paul points out that a true believer has made some very definite commitments.

The Christian needs all the strength and encouragement that only God can give to confess who he or she really is—a person with a new nature, created in the likeness of God.

## Searching the Scriptures

Read **Ephesians 4:17–5:20.**

1. What areas of everyday life are affected by Christ's commitment to you and your response of Christian commitment?

Living the Christian life has two aspects, and both of them require positive action. The first involves a firm opposition to all that is characteristic of the life of one who is not a part of the body of Christ. Paul speaks of this as "[putting] off your old self" **(4:22).** No doubt much of what Paul is saying about impurity of life reflects the fact that drunkenness and certain sexual practices were closely associated with the heathen religions of his day.

2. If Paul were writing today, what do you think he might substitute for "no longer live as the Gentiles do" **(4:17)?** Do you think there might be some relationship between the increasing severity of many social problems today (e.g., dishonesty, greed, violence, sexuality immorality) and the beliefs or "religion" of many today? Explain your answer.

3. Scan **Ephesians 4:17–5:20** again and list the behaviors Paul says are inconsistent with the Christian way of life.

Unfortunately, many people, including Christian people, seem to believe that avoiding evil is all that the Christian life entails. Many Christians as well as non-Christians perceive Christianity as being against something rather than being for something. To say the least, that is certainly a negative view, and it is certainly not what Scripture says. Instead, we desire to do what God desires because of what God has done for us in Christ Jesus. Paul speaks not only of putting off your old self, but also of putting on the new self.

4. What kinds of attitudes and behaviors reflect the commitment a Christian has made?

# The Word for Us

Since Paul says we should have a concern because "we are all members of one body," he is obviously referring to the relationship of members of the church to one another, particularly in the matter of truthfulness (4:25).

1. Is lack of truthfulness a problem for the church today? How does one speak falsehood without telling an outright lie? Do "bitterness, rage and anger, brawling and slander, along with every form of malice" (4:31) ever appear among Christians? Explain your answer.

2. What is St. Paul's Spirit-given advice for such a situation? See **Ephesians 4.26.**

We can never forget that our Christian commitment is a reflection of our faith. We are not saved because of our Christian commitment; we are committed to Christian living because we confess that we have been saved by God's grace.

Dr. C. F. W. Walther once presented the following thesis for discussion:

> God's Word is not rightly divided when faith is pictured either as if merely regarding something as true would justify and save in spite of mortal sins, or as if faith justifies and saves for the sake of the love and renewal it effects (*Law and Gospel*, trans. H. J. A. Bouman, Concordia, 1981, p. 110).

In another thesis he wrote:

> God's Word is not rightly divided when it is suggested that shedding certain vices and performing certain works and virtues is a true conversion (p. 152).

3. What point is Dr. Walther making? Do you agree with his theses? Why or why not?

# Closing

Sing or speak together the words of "Blest the Children of Our God."

Blest the children of our God,
They are bought with Christ's own blood;
They are ransomed from the grave,
Life eternal they will have:
With them numbered may we be
Here and in eternity!

They are justified by grace,
They enjoy the Savior's peace;
All their sins are washed away,
They will stand in God's great day:
With them numbered may we be
Here and in eternity!

They are lights upon the earth,
Children of a heav'nly birth;
One with God, with Jesus one;
Glory is in them begun:
With them numbered may we be
Here and in eternity!

# Lesson 11

# Related!

## Theme Verse

Submit to one another out of reverence for Christ. **Ephesians 5:21**

## Goal

In this session we will seek to better understand and appreciate that our family relationships are grounded in our relationship to Christ and to one another in His church.

## What's Going On Here?

There is a great deal of concern today about the breakdown of traditional family relationships. Today the operative word seems to be *disintegration*—of the family, of civil and domestic values once assumed to be the norm, of the community at large. One out of every two marriages in America ends in divorce. Thousands of children run away from home each year. Thousands more are the victims of neglect or abuse. Greed, dishonesty, and violence appear, it seems, at every turn. "Alternate" lifestyles are being experimented with by many.

How are Christians to react to all of these things—things that threaten the traditional family structure as most of us once knew it? How can we live out our Christian commitment to Christ and His church while living in an age when the very word *family* seems to be taking on a new and different meaning?

## Searching the Scriptures

Paul's words in **Ephesians 5:21–6:4** may provide some answers to the questions in the previous section. His words are directed to Christians who are trying to live their Christian lives within the structure of family that

God ordained. Read Paul's words carefully and note

1. *any words that you feel might be helpful to you as a member of a Christian family;*

2. *any words that you do not understand;*

3. *any words with which you tend to disagree.*

Write a sentence or two that explains why you feel the way you do.

# Be Subject ...

Imagine that you are a first-century Christian. You live at the time of Paul, and you are trying to "live a life worthy of the calling you have received" **(Ephesians 4:1 )**. There are a number of things you will need to consider.

Consider, for example, your position within the family as a husband or wife, son or daughter. If you are a husband, you are definitely the "head of the household." Not only are you the ultimate decision-maker and the one whose responsibility it is to provide for the physical needs of your family, but you are also the protector of your wife and children. Not only that, but as a husband you are the "superior" marriage partner in every sense of the term. You probably paid a "bride price" to your wife's father as part of the marriage contract, thus, in essence, purchasing her to be your possession. Your wife is thought of by you as being among the material goods you have accumulated.

If you are a wife, you take for granted that your position in relation to your husband is one of subservience. While you do have certain duties to perform as the woman of the household, your primary function is to bear children and to provide a male heir for your husband. So important is the role that if for any reason you are unable to fulfill it, your husband can divorce you and marry another or can enter into a sexual relationship with a female servant in order to provide a male heir for himself.

If you are a son or daughter, your filial obligation to your family is absolute. Discipline by your father is rigorous.

If you are a son, you will be raised by your mother until about age 7, when your father will assume responsibility for your education. Over the next years he will guide you on the road to adulthood and on the way to assuming your station in life.

If you are a daughter, your education will continue in the home, where you will be schooled in the management of domestic affairs.

Whether a son or daughter, at some time a marriage will be arranged for you. You will not necessarily have any say in the selection of your spouse.

That is a fairly accurate summary of what marriage and family life was like at Paul's time. Now reread **Ephesians 5:21–33** as though you were a husband or wife at the time of Paul.

1. What new and radical idea is Paul communicating to you?

2. How is Paul suggesting that you change your ideas about your relationship to your husband or wife?

3. According to Paul, what can provide the basis for a new and different kind of marriage relationship?

## For Parents and Children

Read **Ephesians 6:1–4.**

1. What is Paul's command to children?

2. What is Paul's command to fathers?

# The Word for Us

## Be Subject ... Today

You do not, of course, live at the time of Paul. You live at the end of the 20th century, and the shape and structure of marriage today—even Christian marriage—is not the same as it was at the time when Paul wrote this epistle.

1. If you are married is your relationship with your husband or wife similar to that of a husband or wife at Paul's time?

2. How does it differ?

The main idea that Paul is presenting is that the pattern for the relationship between a Christian husband and wife should be the relationship between Christ and His church. As Christ is the head of the church, so should the husband be head of the household. As Christ loved the church and gave Himself for her, so the Christian husband should love his wife with the same self-sacrificing love. The Christian wife should respond to her husband with the same kind of loving sacrifice with which the church responds to Christ.

And now the big question:

3. How does that concept apply to your marriage? Why is this concept important in order to have a healthy marriage?

## For Parents and Children—Today

1. What do the words "in the Lord" **(6:1)** add to the command that children should obey their parents?

2. What do you think is involved in honoring father and mother? Does it, for example, mean agreeing with their decisions at all times? (Explain.)

3. How can parents honor Paul's command, "Fathers, do not exasperate your children" **(6:4)?**

# In Retrospect

Now go back to the sentences you wrote at the beginning of this session. Have you found any other words of Paul helpful now? Do you understand any of Paul's words that you did not understand before? Do you now find yourself agreeing with any of Paul's words with which you disagreed before? Discuss with other participants ways in which Paul's words can help you "live a life worthy of the calling you have received" **(4:1)** in your family relationships.

# To Do This Week

Since the next two sessions will conclude our study of Ephesians, take some time during this coming week to go back through the letter once more. Look especially for those passages next to which you placed question marks in the first session. If your questions have not been answered, raise them for discussion during the final class sessions.

# Closing

Sing or speak together the words of "Oh, Blest the House."

Oh, blest the house, whate'er befall,
Where Jesus Christ is all in all!
For if He were not dwelling there,
How dark and poor and void it were!

Oh, blest that house where faith is found
And all in charity abound
To trust their God and serve Him still
And do in all His holy will!

Oh, blest that house; it prospers well!
In peace and joy the parents dwell,
And in their children's lives is shown
How richly God can bless His own.

Then here will I and mine today
A solemn cov'nant make and say:
Though all the world forsake His Word,
My house and I will serve the Lord.

# Lesson 12

# Employed!

## Theme Verse

Serve wholeheartedly, as if you were serving the Lord. **Ephesians 6:7**

## Goal

In this session we will seek to grow in our understanding and appreciation of the relationship between our Christian faith and our work. We will discover guiding principles for living out our faith in our roles as employers and/or employees.

## What's Going On Here?

"Business is business" is a motto by which many people—even Christian people—live. To such people Christianity is fine, but Christianity and business don't mix. The two seem to be based on principles that are diametrically opposed. Business involves competition, while Christianity involves cooperation and personal concern for others and "never the twain shall meet."

If you were to say that to St. Paul, he would disagree violently. As far as he was concerned, every aspect of life was related to Christian faith. A worker, if she is committed to Christ, is a Christian worker. A businessman, if he is a Christian, is a Christian businessman. Life cannot be divided into "secular" and "religious" life. For a Christian, says St. Paul, all of life is religious.

The Christian employer and the Christian employee are both employed—employed in the service of Christ. This is what governs and directs the behavior of each. That is what St. Paul is saying in **Ephesians 6:5–9.**

# Searching the Scriptures

## Not As Slaves

The economic system at Paul's time was one that, of course, we would not approve of today, since it included the practice of slavery. Although the Bible never directly attacks that practice as being wrong, it undermines the practice of enslaving another human being by introducing the radical idea that all human beings should be treated as people rather than things.

An outstanding example of an approach that would make slavery impossible is found in Paul's letter to Philemon. Philemon was the owner of the slave Onesimus. Onesimus was a slave who had run away and through contact with Paul during Paul's imprisonment had become a Christian.

1. Read **Philemon 8–20.** How do Paul's words to Philemon undermine the practice of slavery?

2. Now read **Ephesians 6:5–9.** How do Paul's words here threaten the traditional master-slave relationship?

## But As Servants of Christ

Although written to slaves and masters, we can discover in Paul's words principles that apply to the employer-employee relationship in our economic system.

1. Write a paraphrase of this section of Ephesians using the words *employers* and *employees* instead of *masters* and *slaves*. List as many principles from Paul's words as you can that would apply to Christian employees and Christian employers today.

2. Paul says that Christians are to do their work "as servants of Christ" (**6:6** RSV). How can that be done? How can one view the activity of providing products or services for people as serving Christ? Christ's words referring to Judgment Day recorded in **Matthew 25:31–46** will give you a clue. What does He say?

It is often difficult today for Christians to view themselves as doing their work "as servants of Christ." This is especially true for the worker on the assembly line or for anyone who works at a job that requires the repetition of the same task hour after hour.

3. How would Paul's words here apply to such a person? What do you think are some of the factors in our economic system that cause people to work as "men-pleasers" (**6:6** RSV)?

4. Is it wrong to do one's work well with a view toward personal gain?

5. Paul points out that "there is no favoritism with [God]" (**6:9**). Look at **Matthew 5:45** and **Romans 3:21–25**. What are some ways in which God shows His impartiality?

6. How has Paul expressed that impartiality in **Ephesians 2:8–10?**

# The Word for Us

Today, as in Paul's day, it is more difficult for a Christian to live out the principles developed in **Ephesians 6:5–9** when the other party is not a Christian.

Imagine that you are involved in a labor-management dispute. The dispute has resulted in a strike. Your class leader will divide your class into two groups, one group to present the case for each side. How will you as a Christian act out your faith in this situation? Explain your answer here.

# Closing

Sing or speak together the words of "O God of Mercy, God of Light."

O God of mercy, God of light,
In love and mercy infinite,
Teach us, as ever in Your sight,
To live our lives in You.

You sent Your Son to die for all
That our lost world might hear Your call;
Oh, hear us lest we stray and fall!
We rest our hope in You.

Teach us the lesson Jesus taught:
To feel for those His blood has bought,
That ev'ry deed and word and thought
May work a work for You.

For all are kindred, far and wide,
Since Jesus Christ for all has died;
Grant us the will and grace provide
To love them all in You.

# Lesson 13

# Armed!

## Theme Verse

Put on the full armor of God so that you can take your stand against the devil's schemes. **Ephesians 6:11**

## Goal

In this session we will by the Spirits' power arm ourselves with the equipment that is ours as soldiers of the faith. We will seek to "put on the full armor of God" so that we can take our stand daily against our Old Adam and against the forces of evil arrayed against us.

## What's Going On Here?

Military terms are a familiar part of our vocabulary. Every nation wants to be prepared to defend itself against potential enemies.

Christians too live in a hostile world. Surrounded by groups with anti-Christian goals, ready to be pounced on by Satan—a "roaring lion" as Peter describes him **(1 Peter 5:8)**—and weakened by the sinful nature that still clings to them, they need all the armament that they can possibly collect in order to win in the daily battle of life. As we will read in this section, our Lord is willing to give us His strength and His power and to arm us for the battle.

St. Paul knew the strength of the enemy forces, and so he wrote to the people of his day and to us to encourage us to be fully armed and ready to fight. His words are found in **Ephesians 6:10–20.**

## Searching the Scriptures

Read **Ephesians 6:10–20.**

It would be frustrating to be engaged in a battle and not know who the enemy is. Many of those involved in the war in Vietnam experienced that kind of situation. They could never be sure who was friend and who was foe. For Christians, the identification of the spiritual enemy is most difficult since the kind of identification made by St. Paul is so foreign to our thought. The forces are superhuman.

1. How do these forces appear in life? Consider, for example, the atrocities committed in war. Is there any relation between the activity of governments and the activities of "the rulers ... authorities ... [and] powers of this dark world" **(6:12)**?

2. How has Satan used the organized church to promote evil? Think of, for example, the Inquisition or the Thirty Years' War. Does anything similar occur today?

3. The tactics of the enemy are clearly described as "the devil's schemes" **(6:11)**. What does that phrase imply?

4. How is Satan described in **2 Corinthians 11:14?** Note also the description of the "lawless one" in **2 Thessalonians 2:9** and the power behind his activity.

Because of our sinful nature, we can easily rationalize and be deceived by things that are evil when they are made to appear good or when they appear to be means by which good goals can be achieved. This can happen both within the church and outside it.

## Put on the Equipment

1. Twice in this section Paul emphasizes "the full armor of God" **(Ephesians 6:11, 13).** Why do you suppose he used that phrase?

2. List the various items designated by St. Paul. What is the specific purpose of each piece of equipment?

Taken all together the "full armor of God" provides a defense against any force that can challenge the Christian. Truth, righteousness, and all the other pieces of armor are gifts of Christ. Putting on "the full armor of God" therefore means putting on Christ. In Christ, we are equipped with all the power that God has to offer.

3. The shield protects the whole person. Paul describes faith as a shield. Doubt is the opposite of faith. How can doubt affect a person's spiritual life?

Once again, the idea of grace is very important, for pride and doubt will destroy faith more quickly than anything else.

4. Paul says, "Take the helmet of salvation" **(6:17).** Is salvation a past, present, or future event or is it all three? Why?

5. If one has salvation, what effect will this have in the battle of life?

6. "The sword of the Spirit, which is the word of God" takes several forms. One form is the written Word **(Matthew 4:1–11).** Another form is the Word of promise in Holy Baptism and in the Lord's Supper, which forgives our sins so Satan cannot successfully accuse us. Does the Word of God spoken by fellow Christians qualify as "the sword of the Spirit"? Explain your answer.

# The Word for Us

One can win a battle and lose the war. In reality, of course, the war has already been won by Christ, and it is only as we remain in faith that we can be assured of victory. For that to occur, we need the presence of the Spirit, and it is certainly fitting that we should pray for His action in our hearts.

1. Read **verse 18** again. To pray, one must be alert. How can one pray "on all occasions"?

2. Is there a limit to this activity when it is necessary to be involved in the day-to-day business of living?

Once again, note that this prayer is not only personal. It is "for all the saints." The church is people bound to each other by their common faith in Christ. They need each other and all need the Spirit. In Christ, together they will conquer.

# Closing

As a fitting conclusion to this study, sing or speak together the words of "Onward, Christian Soldiers."

Onward, Christian soldiers,
Marching as to war,
With the cross of Jesus
Going on before.
Christ, the royal master,
Leads against the foe;
Forward into battle
See His banners go!
*Refrain*
Onward, Christian soldiers,
Marching as to war,
With the cross of Jesus
Going on before.

Like a mighty army
Moves the Church of God;
Brothers, we are treading
Where the saints have trod.
We are not divided,
All one body we,
One in hope and doctrine,
One in charity.
*Refrain*

Crowns and thrones may perish,
Kingdoms rise and wane,
But the Church of Jesus
Constant will remain.
Gates of hell can never
'Gainst that Church prevail;
We have Christ's own promise,
And that cannot fail.
*Refrain*

Onward, then, ye faithful,
Join our happy throng,
Blend with ours your voices

In the triumph song:
Glory, laud, and honor
Unto Christ, the king;
This through countless ages
Men and angels sing.
*Refrain*

# EPHESIANS
## The Church: God's Servant

**Leaders Notes**

# Preparing to Teach Ephesians

Begin your preparation to teach by reading the text of Paul's letter to the Ephesians in a modern translation. The NIV is the translation most often referred to in the lessons of this study.

When you have finished reading the letter itself, we recommend that you consult the introduction to Paul's Captivity Letters and the introduction to Ephesians in the *Concordia Self-Study Commentary*. Read also the introduction to Ephesians in the *Concordia Self-Study Bible*. These three items will supply some basic background information about Ephesians.

If you are interested in additional background material, we recommend three additional books: R. C. H. Lenski's commentary on Ephesians, F. F. Bruce's *New Testament History*, and Merrill C. Tenney's *New Testament Times*.

The latter two volumes offer a perspective on the wider Roman world, and the former offers, in its introduction to Ephesians, a more detailed exposition of the background of Paul's letters. All three volumes may be available through your church library.

Finally, read the text of Paul's letter once again. Then review the study materials in this booklet in preparation for the first session.

In "Searching the Scriptures," the leader guides discussion, using the questions given (or others) to help the class discover what the text actually says. This is a major part of teaching, namely, directing the learners to discover for themselves.

Another major portion of each lesson is "The Word for Us." This section helps participants, through discussion, to see the meaning of the text for our times, for our church and world today, and especially for our own lives.

## Group Bible Study

Group Bible study means mutual learning from one another under the guidance of a leader. The Bible is an inexhaustible resource. No one person can discover all it has to offer. In a class many eyes see many things and can apply them to many life situations. The leader should resist the temptation to "give the answers" and so act as an "authority." This teaching approach stifles participation by individual members and can actually hamper learning. As a general rule the teacher is not to "give interpretation" but to "develop interpreters." Of course there are times when the leader should and must share insights and information gained by his or her own deeper research. The ideal class is one in which the leader guides class members through the lesson and engages them in meaningful sharing and discussion at all points, leading them to a summary of the lesson at the close. As a general rule, don't explain what the learners can discover by themselves.

Have a chalkboard and chalk or newsprint and marker available to emphasize significant points of the lesson. Rephrase your inquiries or the inquiries of participants as questions, problems, or issues. This provokes thought. Keep discussion to the point. List on the chalkboard or newsprint the answers given. Then determine the most vital points made in the discussion. Ask additional questions to fill apparent gaps.

The aim of every Bible study is to help people grow spiritually, not merely in biblical and theological knowledge, but in Christian thinking and living. This means growth in Christian attitudes, insights, and skills for Christian living. The focus of this course must be the church and the world of our day. The guiding question will be this: What does the Lord teach us for life today through Paul's letter to the Ephesians?

## Pace Your Teaching

Depending on the time you have, you may not want to cover every question in each lesson. This may lead to undue haste and frustration. Be selective. Pace your teaching. Spend no more than 5–10 minutes with "Theme Verse," "Goal," and "What's Going On Here?" Take time to go into the text by topic, but not word by word. Get the sweep of meaning. Occasionally stop to help the class gain understanding of a word or concept. Allow approximately 10–15 minutes for "The Word for Us." Allowing approximately 5 minutes for "Closing" and announcements, you will notice, allows you only approximately 30 minutes for "Searching the Scriptures."

Should your group have more than a one-hour class period, you can take it more leisurely. But do not allow any lesson to drag and become tiresome. Keep it moving. Keep it alive. Keep it meaningful. Eliminate some questions and restrict yourself to those questions most meaningful to the members of the class. If most members study the text at home, they can report their findings, and the time gained can be applied to relating the lesson to life.

## Good Preparation

Good preparation by the leader usually affects the pleasure and satisfaction the class will experience.

## Suggestions to the Leader for Using the Study Guide

### The Lesson Pattern

This set of 13 lessons is based on a timely New Testament book—Ephesians. The material is designed to aid *Bible study*, that is, to aid a consideration of the written Word of God, with discussion and personal application growing out of the text at hand.

The typical lesson is divided into these sections:

1. Theme Verse
2. Goal
3. What's Going On Here?
4. Searching the Scriptures
5. The Word for Us
6. Closing

"Theme Verse," "Goal," and "What's Going On Here?" give the leader assistance in arousing the interest of the group in the concepts of the lesson. Here the leader stimulates minds. Do not linger too long over the introductory remarks.

"Searching the Scriptures" provides the real spadework necessary for Bible study. Here the class digs, uncovers, and discovers; it gets the facts and observes them. Comments from the leader are needed only to the extent that they help the group understand the text. The same is true of looking up the indicated parallel passages. The questions in this guide, arranged under subheadings and corresponding to sections within the text, are intended to help the participants discover the meaning of the text.

Having determined what the text says, the class is ready to apply the message. Having heard, read, marked, and learned the Word of God, proceed to digest it inwardly through discussion, evaluation, and application. This is done, as this guide suggests, by taking the truths found in Ephesians and applying them to the world and Christianity, in general, and then to personal Christian life. Class time may not permit discussion of all questions and topics. In preparation the leader may need to select one or two and focus on them. These questions bring God's message to the individual Christian. Close the session by reviewing one important truth from the lesson.

Remember, the Word of God is sacred, but this study guide is not. The notes in this section offer only guidelines and suggestions. Do not hesitate to alter the guidelines or substitute others to meet your needs and the needs of the participants. Adapt your teaching plan to your class and your class period. Good teaching directs the learner to discover for himself or herself. For the teacher this means directing the learner, not giving the learner answers. Choose the verses that should be looked up in Scripture. What discussion questions will you ask? At what points? Write them in the margin of your study guide. Involve class members, but give them clear directions. What practical actions might you propose for the week following the lesson? Which of the items do you consider most important for your class?

How will you best use your teaching period? Do you have 45 minutes? an hour? or an hour and a half? If time is short, what should you cut? Learn to become a wise steward of class time.

Be sure to take time to summarize the lesson, or have a class member do it. Plan brief opening and closing devotions, using members of the class. In addition, remember to pray frequently for yourself and your class.

# Lesson 1
## A Letter from a Friend

### Before the Session

Take time to read Paul's letter to the Ephesians. You may also find it helpful to read the rest of Paul's Captivity Letters: Philippians, Colossians, and Philemon. Review "Preparing to Teach Ephesians." Finally, remember that you do not need to know all the answers, but the class will look to you as a resource person for their discussions.

Provide the map you will use in "Searching the Scriptures."

### Getting Started

Before you begin your study of Ephesians, be sure class members know one another. Take a few moments for introductions if they do not. Even if they are acquainted, it might be helpful to have each participant tell one interesting fact about himself or herself—a hobby, an interest, a concern, etc., that other participants may not be aware of. Since this course will be a study of the church, it will be helpful to know something about those who make up the church in your congregation and to create a comfortable fellowship among participants.

### The Class Session

After an opening prayer and a brief check to see that everyone has a Bible, ask a member of the class to read aloud "Theme Verse," "Goal," and What's Going On Here?" Ask for questions or comments.

Have students work individually or in pairs to paraphrase **Eph. 2:10.** Take time for them to share these paraphrases with the class.

The letter to the Ephesians can be divided into two major sections. **Chapters 1–3** are *doctrinal;* that is, they deal with the essential teachings of our Christian faith. **Chapters 4–6** are *practical.* **Eph. 2:10** provides a summary of the letter. This verse speaks of God's action in creating the church for good works **(chapters 1–3)** and *our response to God's action by performing the good works that God has provided for us* **(chapters 4–6).**

**Eph. 2:10** describes the church in terms of its origin, nature, and purpose. The church is created by God to do the good works that God has prepared beforehand for it. Its members need not search for good works to perform. They need only seize the opportunities that are before them.

# Searching the Scriptures

Read aloud, or have a participant read aloud, the opening paragraph of this section. In each of the subsections that follow, have participants first read aloud the introductory material and then answer the questions.

## Who

The recipients of this letter are difficult to identify. Some passages seem to imply that Paul was not well acquainted with them (**3:2; 4:21**). If the letter was written to the church in Ephesus, this is difficult to understand, since Paul spent much time there.

1. Both this letter and the letter to the Colossians were to be delivered by Tychicus (**Eph. 6:21; Col. 4:7**). Some Bible scholars believe that Ephesians is the letter to the Laodiceans (**Col. 4:16**) and was later ascribed to Ephesus because Ephesus was the principal city in that area. None of this can be verified. Do not allow the discussion to get bogged down over this issue or over the various issues raised in the introduction. The central focus of the letter is the church, and the problems dealt with in the letter are universal.

2. The churches named in **Rev. 1:11** are Ephesus, Smyrna, Pergamum, Thyatira, Sardis, Philadelphia, and Laodicea.

3. For the map activity you will need a map showing Ephesus and surrounding congregations at the time of Paul. A map of Paul's second missionary journey would be ideal. Have participants locate Ephesus and the congregations identified in **Rev. 1:11** on the map.

## When

1. Paul stopped in Ephesus near the end of his second missionary journey and for a short time reasoned with the Jews in the synagogue. Paul left Priscilla and Aquila in Ephesus, and they instructed Apollos, who spoke with great fervor about Jesus.

2. Paul proclaimed the Gospel of Jesus boldly and persuasively, first in the synagogue and then in the lecture hall of Tyrannus. This he did for two years.

## Where

While we do not know the city from which Paul wrote this letter, we do know that it was written while Paul was in prison (**Eph. 3:1, 13; 4:1; 6:18–20**). Whether this imprisonment was in Ephesus itself (see **1 Cor. 15:32; 2 Cor. 11:23**), Caesarea (**Acts 23:23–26:32**), or Rome (**Acts 28:16–20**) is not revealed by Scripture.

## Why

No matter where Paul was imprisoned, he apparently had the opportunity to meditate on the nature and purpose of the church and was led by the Holy Spirit to write this letter in order to help members of the congregation addressed consider questions of who they were as Christians, how they came to be Christians, and what was expected of them as Christians.

1. In his farewell address to the Ephesian elders, Paul says that imprisonment and afflictions await him and that he will not return to Ephesus. These statements may indicate why Paul later wrote this letter to the congregations that he had established or had helped establish in and around Ephesus.

2. Paul warns his friends that dangers—"savage wolves" (**Acts 20:29**)—await them and that they are to keep alert.

3. Paul commits his friends "to God and to the word of His grace" (**Acts 20:32**), which has the power to build them up and to carry them through the trials that await them.

## The Word for Us

Discuss one or more of the questions in this section. If your group is large, you may wish to divide into small groups of three or four to discuss the questions.

Remind everyone that these questions are not designed as opportunities to point fingers or engage in gossip and backbiting. Instead, they are designed to help us recognize that, in spite of sometimes overwhelming problems, we too can find comfort and strength in God and in "the word of His grace" (**Acts 20:32**), which can carry us through our struggles today and to the glorious future of eternal life with Him.

1–3. Answers will vary. In so many ways, we can say that the "wolves" who today seek to destroy the flock are the same as those who sought to destroy the young Ephesian church: the temptations, animosity, and hatred of the world on one hand and on the other false doctrine, pride, and divisiveness from within the church itself.

4. We find our comfort in God and "the word of His grace," as previously noted.

5. Encourage participants to complete this activity.

## To Do This Week

Encourage participants to read all of Paul's letter to the Ephesians this week. Encourage them to use the symbols described to make their reading more meaningful and to help prepare them for further discussion. Urge those who have some familiarity with this letter to approach it as though they had never read it before. In this way they may receive new insights into the message of Ephesians.

## Closing

Sing or pray together "O Word of God Incarnate."

# Lesson 2
## Chosen!

### Getting Started

As the class gathers, meet and greet participants. If any are present who did not attend lesson 1, welcome these newcomers and introduce them to other class members.

If you have a recording of "Amazing Grace," play it softly as the group gathers. If enough participants are familiar with this hymn, sing it as an opening devotion.

### The Class Session

After an opening prayer and a brief check to see that everyone has a Bible, ask a member of the class to read aloud "Theme Verses," "Goal," and What's Going On Here?" Then allow participants a minute or two to answer the question. Invite volunteers to share their answers. Do not insist that "volunteers" do so, though.

Often in life we make many of our choices because of some advantage for us or attraction to us in the person or object chosen.

### Searching the Scriptures

Have participants read **Eph. 1:3–4.** Allow them a few minutes to take the quiz. Do not discuss their answers at this time.

After participants have read **Eph. 2:8–9,** let them decide whether they wish to change any answers to the quiz. Now talk about the quiz. The only statement that should be marked true is "God chose us because of His grace in Jesus Christ."

Many people, even church members, find it hard to give God all the credit He deserves. As the saying goes, "We always want to put our sticky fingers into the matter of our salvation." Even members of the church find themselves constantly comparing themselves to those who appear to be less acceptable than they are either because of their actions or their personal characteristics. "Before the creation of the world" **(1:4)** makes it perfectly clear that our position as members of the church has nothing to do with our actions and characteristics. God chose us. His choice is due entirely to His grace.

1. *Grace* is God's undeserved favor. It always involves free action on His part as He gives or does something. To have been chosen by God's grace means that we cannot make claims of any kind on God. He chose us even before we came into existence. We were not chosen because we are special, but we are special because we have been chosen.

2. Have participants count the number of phrases that appear in **1:3–14** that refer to our salvation "in Christ."

3. Have participants read **John 1:17** and discuss the question. God's action of grace is always "in Christ," because He is the one through whom God's love comes to us. God's demands and requirements are apparent from His Law, and His wisdom and power can be seen in nature, but only in *Christ* does His grace appear. Apart from Christ, God is not known as the saving God. St. Paul emphasizes this also in **Titus 2:11,** which is part of the letter read at Christmas in many congregations. In this verse the appearance of Christ for the salvation of all is described as "the grace of God."

## The Word for Us

Read the opening paragraph of this section; then allow participants to answer the questions.

1–2. The main point should be that one who is chosen to a desired position feels gratitude toward those who have chosen him or her.

3. Have participants individually or in pairs complete their word lists from this portion of Ephesians, then create their own expressions of praise and thanks to God. Either at this time or during your closing devotions, ask volunteers to share their statements of praise and thanks.

4. While it is only in Christ that the grace of God can be seen, we could not see God's grace apart from the sending of the Son by the Father or the faith-giving work of the Holy Spirit. In the rereading of **1:3–14,** participants will discover that Paul praises "the God and Father of our Lord Jesus Christ" for choosing us in Christ **(vv. 3–4)** and for our being "sealed with the promised Holy Spirit" **(v. 13** RSV).

5. In Luther's explanation to the Third Article, he has clearly and concisely stated that our salvation from beginning to end is God's work "lest any man should boast" **(Eph. 2:9** RSV). In Christ we have the assurance of forgiveness of sins and eternal life.

## Closing

Follow the suggestions outlined in this section of lesson 2.

# Lesson 3

## Created!

### Getting Started

Since the letter to the Ephesians is about the church and the care and concern of the members for each other, it would be appropriate to ask about any participants who may be missing today and to have those who are present share any joyful experiences and/or problems they may have had during the past week. These could be woven into an opening prayer, or each class member could be asked to form his or her own one-sentence prayer concerning experiences of the past week.

### The Class Session

Begin with prayer. See the suggestion above. Briefly review with the class the concept discussed last week, being chosen by God's grace. Point out that in today's session we will be discussing how God brings those whom He has chosen by His grace out of the nothingness of death into fullness of life.

Ask for a volunteer to read "Theme Verse," "Goal," and "What's Going On Here?"

### Searching the Scriptures

Have participants look up the passages and discuss the questions.

1. In each of the passages listed, God is presented as the only Creator. He is the original Creator of physical life, and also the Creator of our new life as we confess in the Apostles' Creed. **Gen. 1:1** tells us that God created the heavens and the earth. **Gen. 1:3** relates that God created light out of nothing by His powerful word. The Spirit of God is described in **Psalm 104** as essential to the physical life of all things. In **Isaiah 43,** God is identified as the Creator of the people of Israel, and in **Ps. 51:10,** it is God who creates a clean heart. In **Col. 1:15–16,** Christ is described as the firstborn of all creation and the one through whom everything else is brought into being. **2 Cor. 5:17–18** most clearly points out that the believer is a new

creation in Christ.

2. In all of these passages, the subject of the word *create* is God, who brings into existence something that was not there before. Thus our creation in Christ Jesus is God's act of bringing into being something that did not previously exist.

If time permits, participants might also examine **Ezek. 37:1–14.** This vision is a vivid picture of God's creative action. The dry bones are lifeless until the breath, wind, Spirit (these three words all translate the same Hebrew word) of God causes them to live.

3. The human condition is as bleak and parched and lifeless as Ezekiel's valley of dry bones. Humanity follows the "ways of this world" and the "ruler of the kingdom of the air." By nature we are dead in sin and evil.

4. The phrases "cravings of our sinful nature" and "its desires and thoughts" are fairly obvious. **Rom. 1:18–32** is a catalog of perverted and depraved behavior.

A more subtle concept can also be found in "desires and thoughts": Some people seek to find *their* answers to life in human intellect rather than in "what may be known about God" **(Rom. 1:19).** Although perhaps no longer as true as it once was, it is still a popular view that the solution to human problems lies in the "unlimited" capacity of the human mind, aided by humankind's "creation" of modern technology.

A more modern spin on this focus on self rather than God can be found in various human-potential movements, where "getting in touch with oneself" is touted as the medicine for humanity's assorted ills.

Many serious-minded people, however, recognize that the things accomplished by people and their products, or by people and their minds, still result in death. The problem lies within people; the solution does not.

5. Have participants discuss the phrases. These phrases, of course, appeal to the "cravings of our sinful nature." If we take Paul seriously, we probably should not use these phrases.

## The Word for Us

Read the introduction to this section, then have participants read **Eph. 2:4–10** and **John 3:16–17** and answer the questions.

1. God has re-created us as His new beings because of His mercy, love, and grace. Our re-creation is His free gift.

2. God sent His Son into the world for our salvation. It is through Him that we are created for fullness of life.

3. **Rom. 6:3–4** says that we are brought from death to life as we are united with the death and resurrection of Christ. Luther's words point out that it is God who delivers us from death and that His re-creation is not a one-

time action but a daily occurrence.

The purpose of God's re-creative activity is that we might "live before God in righteousness and purity forever." You may wish to point out the parallel between Luther's words and Paul's words in **Eph. 2:6–7.**

## Closing

Sing "Baptized into Your Name Most Holy." Before singing this hymn, spend a few minutes discussing what the hymn says about our being brought from death to life.

# Lesson 4

## Transferred!

## Getting Started

Hopefully, the members of your group have become close-knit by now, willing to share their thoughts and feelings, including any feelings of doubt, discouragement, or failure. Since it is part of the task of church members to strengthen one another, you might begin today's session with an opening prayer led by one of the members of the group. This prayer might include problems or concerns that have been shared with the class. It might be a good idea to ask someone several days before this session to accept this responsibility, so that he or she has an opportunity for thought and preparation.

## The Class Session

Open the session with a prayer (see above). Have a volunteer read "Theme Verses" and "Goal" for this session; then read, or have a volunteer read, "What's Going On Here?"

Do not discuss the story at this time. Move on to "Searching the Scriptures."

## Searching the Scriptures

Read the introductory paragraph.

Paul describes Satan as "the ruler of the kingdom of the air" and "the spirit who is now at work in those who are disobedient." This is not a pre-scientific statement reflecting the belief that somehow evil spirits lurk in the air controlling the lives of people. It is rather a reference to the fact that Satan is present and active in the affairs of this world and in those activities that are opposed to God. The phrase "when you followed the ways of this world" is a reference to that complete and utter corruption that is a characteristic of humanity since the fall into sin. Recall the following phrase in the baptismal rite: "This child … is also by nature sinful and under the wrath of God."

1–3. Satan is no figment of the imagination. **Mark 4:15** presents him as the one who prevents the Word of God from growing in the hearts of some involved in the sickness of humanity. **Luke 13:10–17** identifies him as a cause of physical illness in the world. In **John 13:26–27,** it is Satan who enters the heart of Judas so that he betrays Jesus. **Acts 5:1–4** shows Satan as the cause of Ananias and Sapphira's hypocrisy. And in **1 Cor. 7:5,** Paul says that Satan can use human passions to cause marriage partners to be unfaithful to each other.

4. The ultimate control that Satan holds over people is the universal fear of death, according to **Heb. 2:14–15.** This fear of death causes people to seek security in things that have no lasting value, which ultimately are limited by becoming outdated, impossible to achieve, or no longer desirable. You might ask the group for examples that fit one or more of these categories. Death is the end of all the things that we desire and in which we seek security apart from God.

## The Word for Us

Read the introductory paragraph; then have participants study **Eph. 2:6–10** and answer the questions.

1. Christians are not under the power of the "ruler of the kingdom of the air." Having been made alive in Christ, we are in His care. To be in the kingdom of Christ means to be under His control, to have access to His power and protection, and to be His loyal subjects. The "heavenly realms" are neither some ethereal place nor something in the future, but they are our present situation as members of Christ's kingdom. We live *even now* in eternal life with Him, although the full realization of that life is reserved for the future. The result of our transfer into His kingdom is eternal life with Him that future ages may know "the incomparable riches of His grace" **(2:7).**

2. Our response is to walk in the good works that God has prepared for us **(2:10).**

3. The original readers had been aliens because they were Gentiles and therefore excluded from and, for the most part, unaware of God's covenant promise to Israel. They also had been aliens because they had not been members of God's kingdom and therefore had none of the rights

or privileges that such membership provides. Thus they were aliens both in relation to the community of Israel and in relation to the kingdom of God. The result of that alienation was that they had no hope and were "without God in the world" (2:12). That is the lot of all of us apart from Christ.

4. By God's grace we have been transferred from being aliens to being citizens of Christ's kingdom. The price that Christ paid to make us citizens was His blood shed on the cross (2:13, 16).

5. As citizens we are privileged to be fellow citizens with all other believers and to be joined with them into a dwelling place for God (2:19–22). Our responsibilities are, in a sense, the same as our privileges. It is our responsibility by the power of the Spirit within us to be "a holy temple" (2:21).

6. Answers will vary. This question applies the doctrinal content of this section of Ephesians to the practical situation of the believer. How can we, in the situation and location where God has placed each one of us, exercise our heavenly citizenship? What is our specific role as we join with all the saints to be "a holy temple"? These questions should provide much food for thought and discussion. Encourage participants to be as specific as they can.

7. Answers will vary. Invite participants to share openly.

## Closing

Before singing/speaking this hymn, spend a few minutes discussing what the hymn says about the privileged position of those who have been transferred into the kingdom of Christ.

# Lesson 5
## Primed for Prayer and Praise

## Getting Started

As the group gathers for this session, you might ask if anyone has celebrated a birthday or an anniversary during the past week or will soon be celebrating one. An opening prayer might include thanksgiving for these blessings as well as for the greater blessing of God in bringing the group together in Christ to share their joys and sorrows with one another.

# The Class Session

Begin the class session again today by having participants read "Theme Verses," "Goal," and "What's Going On Here?"

Because many Christians have been Christians all their lives, it is sometimes difficult for them to relate to the conversion experience of Paul. The adult convert to Christianity may often relate better to Paul's experience.

If there are adult converts to Christianity in your class, perhaps they would be willing to share with the class what they see as the change that has taken place in their lives. Every Christian has the same reason to rejoice and to celebrate his or her changed situation.

# Searching the Scriptures

Read the opening paragraph.

## Remember

1. Among the remembrances that moved Paul to celebrate were these: remembrance of having been chosen by God **(1:4)**; remembrance of redemption in Christ **(1:7, 13)**; remembrance of Christ's resurrection and ascension **(1:20).**

2. After participants have identified the remembrances that moved Paul to celebrate, have them list remembrances from their own lives that move them to celebrate. These will probably include Baptism, confirmation, etc., but may also include such things as an especially moving sermon, a Scripture verse spoken by a friend, or an experience at a retreat.

## Praise

Have participants read the introductory paragraph for this section. Then discuss the questions.

1–2. For some reason, many Christians seem reluctant to express their feelings of joy and thanksgiving. They seem embarrassed by friends whose conversation regularly includes words and phrases such as *Hallelujah, praise the Lord, amen,* etc. While it is true that these words can often become almost meaningless phrases thoughtlessly used, no one should automatically come to the conclusion that those who use them are phony and insincere.

If these words or phrases are not suitable for us, we need to discover our own expressions of praise. If we find that we use none, that raises the more serious question, why? and requires our consideration of whether the reason is lack of words, lack of gratitude, fear, etc.

### Thanks

Have participants read the introductory material; then ask them to take a few moments to individually make a list of people for whom they wish to thank God.

### Pray

A look at the past can hardly avoid a look at the future. For while one can be grateful for previous conditions and experiences, the future is yet to be lived. That is why Paul brings his requests for the church to God. It is interesting and significant to note the scope of Paul's requests. They cover the entire church, not only the needs of Paul or even the needs of the congregation or congregations addressed in this letter.

## The Word for Us

Read the introductory paragraph. Have the class answer the questions. Use the quotations to lead the class into a discussion of the scope of prayer concerns. Too often our prayers are limited to personal concerns, local congregational concerns, or denominational concerns rather than concern for the needs of the whole church.

## To Do This Week

Follow the directions in this section of the lesson.

## Closing

Follow the suggestion.

# Lesson 6

## Guaranteed!

## Getting Started

As the group gathers, try to engage participants in conversation about their plans for the days or weeks ahead and possibly about their long-range plans and goals. As the conversation progresses, you might inject a questioning note about what the certainty is that what has been planned will actually come to pass. Then point out that there is a future that is absolutely certain, and that it is that future that we will discuss in today's session.

# The Class Session

Read "Theme Verses" for this lesson. Then have a participant read the remaining introductory paragraphs in this section of the guide. Discuss briefly the three related questions in the last paragraph of "What's Going On Here?"

## Searching the Scriptures

1. In spite of a clear and objective view of his failures and weaknesses, Paul always says, "I am convinced." He was positive that nothing could separate him from God's love in Christ (**Rom. 8:31–38**) and that Christ would guard his eternal future, the future that Paul had completely entrusted to Him (**2 Tim. 1:12**). Paul was certain that the Thessalonian Christians would be found sound and blameless at the coming of Christ (**1 Thess. 5:23–24**) and that the peace of God would guard the hearts and minds of the Philippian believers (**Phil. 4:7**).

Many Christians do not make the same powerfully certain statements as Paul about their future destiny. Responses to questions about their eternal destiny are often couched in phrases that express uncertainty.

2. Have participants read through the anecdote about the man in the train station, then do the activity that asks them to consider what words they would use to answer the man's question about their eternal destiny.

If your class has become an open, sharing group by now, use this activity as a class activity. Otherwise it might be best to have participants work through this activity individually, since their answers will reveal a great deal about their faith.

None of the phrases listed supply a true answer to the question. Put simply, as Christians we can answer emphatically, "I am going to heaven" or "I am going to be with God."

It is important for the Christian to be aware of his or her reasons for answers to the basic questions of life. There is a world of difference between a personal opinion and a personal conviction. It involves the difference between being aware of facts and agreeing with them and trusting that these facts are true *for you* beyond question. The Holy Spirit works mightily through God's Word to strengthen a Christian's faith so he or she can live each day with the assurance that Jesus won for him or her eternal life when He suffered and died on the cross.

3–4. Have class members look at **Eph. 1:11–14.** Our inheritance is our future with God both in this life and in the life to come. The Holy Spirit guarantees our inheritance as we hear the Gospel.

5–6. In the matter of our eternal destiny, it is God who speaks and acts. Our assurance is in Him. The guarantee that His words of promise can be trusted is that they are back up by His mighty acts. For Paul these mighty acts included creation **(Rom. 1:20)**; God's mighty acts in the history of Israel **(1 Cor. 10:1–5)**; His mighty acts in Paul's own life **(Acts 9)**; and most especially, the death and resurrection of Jesus Christ **(Acts 2:22–24)**.

## The Word for Us

1. Through the mighty acts of God in Holy Baptism and the Lord's Supper and through the Word of God, the Holy Spirit continually guarantees us of Christ's death and resurrection for us. It is for this reason that the Holy Spirit is described as our "guarantee." As He works through God's Word, He points us to the promises of God, promises backed up fully by His mighty acts. The faith created and sustained by the Holy Spirit makes our future absolutely certain.

2. The Holy Spirit guarantees our inheritance by pointing us to Christ **(2 Cor. 1:18–22)** and by assuring us that our God has prepared for us a time when "what is mortal may be swallowed up by life" **(2 Cor. 5:4–5)**, that is, a time when our physical life will end, and we shall enter eternal life with Him forever.

## Closing

If time permits, have participants recall as many of God's promises as they can that assure them of eternal life. Use these recollections to construct a prayer of thanksgiving.

Or have the class examine and discuss the stanzas of "O Holy Spirit, Enter In."

# Lesson 7

## Revealed!

## Getting Started

After the group has gathered, lead it in a prayer. Ask for the guidance of God's Holy Spirit during the lesson. Thank God for His protecting presence during the past week and for making it possible for us to have joyful and confident lives because His assurance of our salvation.

# The Class Session

Read "Theme Verses" and "Goal" for this lesson. Then have a participant read the introductory paragraphs in "What's Going On Here?"

## Searching the Scriptures

Mention that in the Christian faith we discern many mysteries. Among them are the mystery of the Trinity, of the incarnation, and of the Lord's Supper. Perhaps the class can think of others. Do not become sidetracked by a discussion of each of them, however, even though such a discussion could be interesting and profitable.

The universality of God's plan of salvation was once included among the mysteries of God. Before the creation of the world, God had conceived that plan **(Eph. 1:4).** He knew its outcome, but it only became clear to people as it was fulfilled.

1. Help the class list incidents that reveal more and more of what God was up to, how His plan of salvation was being fulfilled. Note, for example, the choice of *Abraham, Isaac, Jacob, Judah,* and *David* to be ancestors of the Messiah. Note also the choice of Israel to be bearer of the covenant promises, but ultimately to be a people destined to proclaim God's plan of salvation among the Gentiles.

2. Answers will vary. Even when we come to the events of the New Testament, God's plan is not immediately clear.

It is, of course, clear to us now, but for some time Jesus' disciples did not fully comprehend what was happening. Just prior to His ascension they were still looking for the establishment of the physical kingdom of Israel and wanted to know if this was the time for its restoration **(Acts 1:6–8).**

After Pentecost they had to be pushed beyond the bounds of limiting the Gospel to the nation of Israel. It took a special vision from God to send Peter to the house of the Gentile Cornelius **(Acts 10).** Perhaps this is not too difficult to understand if we read statements such as those in Matthew, directing the disciples not to go among the Gentiles or Samaritans, as well as Christ's statement that He was sent to the lost sheep of the house of Israel.

It was hard for the disciples to put that together with some of His other words that spoke of salvation for all. The Holy Spirit enabled them to understand. Jesus promised to send the Counselor to teach them all things, remind them of everything Jesus said, and guide them into all truth.

3. Jesus spoke of God's love for the world and of salvation for all who believed in Him **(John 3:14–17).** After healing the centurion's servant at Capernaum, He spoke of people coming from all over to fellowship with

the patriarchs (**Matt. 8:5–12**). In a parable, He pointed out that if God's salvation was rejected, it would be given to others (**Matt. 21:33–41**). Before His ascension He commanded His disciples to make disciples of all nations (**Matt. 28:18–20**).

4. Answers will vary. The Holy Spirit made it clear that Christ was for all.

5. The key to the revelation of the mystery was Christ, who was born, lived, died, and rose from the dead for all *people*.

6–7. **Eph. 3:5** points out that God's plan was revealed by the Holy Spirit, and the account in Acts of the spread of the Gospel supports this. The Holy Spirit leads Philip to the Ethiopian and leads Peter to Cornelius. It is the Spirit who directs the church to choose and send out the first missionaries to the Gentiles. Through the action of the Holy Spirit, God revealed the solution to the mystery.

8. God desires all people to receive His gift of salvation.

## The Word for Us

Lead the class in a discussion of the questions posed in this section. As you consider the words and actions of the church today, bring out the point that we speak of salvation for all, but often our actions contradict what we say we believe. If they did not, there would be no hint of segregation in congregations; no lack of resources to seize the opportunities to carry out mission work; no upper-, middle-, and lower-class worship groups.

Do not limit the discussion, but if time permits, discuss the three statements in this section.

The statement that mission work begins at home may be true but can never be used by Christians to excuse their lack of outreach to those of different cultures or nations.

The local congregation is God's church *in this place* and as such has a commitment to serve all people.

Fellowship within the church is always a personal fellowship and our personal relationship with others is an integral part of our Christian mission. Christian love overcomes all divisions among people, just as Christ's love broke down all barriers between God and people and between people of various races and nations (**Eph. 2:14**).

## Closing

Close with the prayer printed in this section of the lesson.

# Lesson 8
## United!

### Before the Session
1. Take a large picture of a church and glue it on cardboard. When the glue dries cut the picture into as many parts as there are members of your study group. Cut it in such a way that the pattern for putting it back together again will be obvious.

2. Review the introductory remarks in "The Class Session" and "Searching the Scriptures." This session marks a transition from the first three chapters of Ephesians to the last three chapters of Paul's letter and a shift from matters of doctrine to those of practical living.

### Getting Started
As members of your study group arrive, give each member a part of the "puzzle" you have created. Ask him or her to keep it for the present. Do not tell them what you plan to do at this time.

After the group has assembled, ask members to join in singing or speaking "The Church's One Foundation." Follow this opening activity with a prayer. Ask the Holy Spirit to lead you to a deeper understanding of the Word that you will study in this session.

Now reassemble the picture. Ask each member of the class to bring forward his or her piece of the puzzle. The point of the activity is that the Christian church gives the appearance of being all broken up, but it is really one unit—united by Christ the crucified, risen, and ascended Savior.

### The Class Session
Read "Theme Verse" for the lesson. Ask for a volunteer to read "Goal" and "What's Going On Here?" Ask for additional volunteers to read the three passages from Ephesians. Discuss the passages briefly before moving on to the next section.

### Searching the Scriptures
While the first portion of Ephesians **(chapters 1–3)** is primarily doctrinal in nature, and we are now considering **Eph. 4:1–6** (the beginning of that portion of Paul's letter that is usually considered the practical section of the letter), there is a close relationship between the two portions. This is apparent in Paul's use of the word *body* which he uses as a synonym for "the church." For that reason in this lesson we will also be considering

**Eph. 2:11–3:6** and **1:22–23,** sections in which the word *body* appears.

1. Jews and Gentiles were hostile toward one another. Paul recognized this and so stressed the peace that had been brought about by Christ. This was especially meaningful to the Gentiles, whom Paul describes as formerly "without hope and without God in the world" **(2:12).** The Jewish people, God's chosen ones, had "the covenants of the promise" **(2:12).** Circumcision, which distinguished the Jews from the Gentiles, was part of the covenant. Christ, however, made peace between God and the members of both groups by means of His death on the cross. This peace was accomplished by Christ's fulfillment of the Law and by His suffering the penalty deserved by all people for their sin. Christ's reconciliation of Jews and Gentiles to God has implications for their reconciliation with each other, as we will see.

2. The reason for the brokenness in the world is the enmity (antagonism) that is present in it because of sin. Sin is the cause of the enmity between God and people and is the source of the problems that exist between people.

3. Answers will vary. Still today people fail to recognize that there is no need for competition with others in order to prove superiority and to assure their own security, since real security is found through God in Christ.

4. Answers will vary. The fact that access to God is a gift of God through Christ, who has brought peace and unites all the members of His body, needs to be proclaimed. The church must be very careful to avoid erecting walls of hostility by excluding or dividing people over issues such as how they dress, how much money they give (or don't give) to the church, and what socioeconomic or ethnic group they are a part of.

5. It is interesting to note the important part that peace plays in the life of Christ. It is proclaimed at His birth, in the chorus the angels sing **(Luke 2:14).** In His resurrection appearance to the disciples gathered behind locked doors, His first words are "Peace be with you! … As the Father has sent Me, I am sending you" **(John 20:19, 21).** These words are followed by His promise of the Holy Spirit and the commission to proclaim forgiveness of sins. Christ's peace is the assurance of forgiveness of sins and eternal life.

6. A proclamation of peace involves the end of enmity between God and people and between people. By it they are brought together. The word *one* emphasizes this as it appears at least 11 times in chapters 2 and 4 in the description of the church.

7. Paul states unequivocally that the church is one, not that it ought to be, might be, or will be. In Christ, the two opposing groups—Jew and Gen-

tile—had been brought together into *one* body. This had been accomplished through the operation of the *one* Spirit who had called them to the *one* same hope of eternal life. The *one* Lord Jesus Christ was the object of their *one* common faith. They all had been baptized in His name and through this had all become children of God, the heavenly Father. The church is one.

Unfortunately, because of sin, the unity that is really there between the members of the body is not always apparent. The Holy Spirit works through the Gospel to bring unity. God's love for us in Christ melts prejudicial attitudes and enables us to embrace all no matter who they are, what they have done, what they look like, or their ethnic background.

8. The basis for that unity was referred to earlier in this letter in the description of the foundation and cornerstone of the church **(2:19–22).** The Word of God, which has come through the apostles and prophets, is the foundation on which the church is established. As its cornerstone, Christ upholds the church and gives it direction for growth.

In building ancient buildings there was always an attempt to find a stone or cut a stone with the outer edge at perfect 90-degree angles. This would assure the builder that the walls of the building would be straight and thus control the direction the building would take. Since cornerstones no longer serve the same function in buildings today, it is important to note their importance for upholding the building and controlling construction in ancient times in order to fully understand Paul's imagery.

9. Both pictures that Paul uses for the church, that of a *body* and that of a *temple* are important. The body with its interdependence of parts in a living organism points to the unity of the church under the leadership of Christ. The body is never without the head and every member is important. The temple too has its interdependent parts, the most important of which is the cornerstone. When Paul describes the church as the temple of God, he is emphasizing the thought that God by His Spirit dwells permanently in the church.

10. This question is related to question 9. It follows, then, from what we have discussed, that if we are to find Christ today, He will be found in His church, in the people who confess Jesus Christ as Lord and Savior.

## The Word for Us

1. By describing the equality of Jews and Gentiles in the church with three phrases, "heirs together with Israel, members together of one body, and sharers together in the promise in Christ Jesus," Paul emphasizes the unity God has brought about through Jesus Christ. One may inherit something but not be a member of the family, or one may be a member of the

family but not inherit an equal share with the other members. So Paul uses all three phrases to emphasize the absolute unity of all members of the church no matter who they are.

2–3. Answers will vary. We need to give more than lip service to the fact that we are "members together of one body." In our practice we need to be careful that we do not give a different impression. For example, one does not become a member of the church at confirmation but has been one since Baptism. And just because one becomes a member of the church later in life, that does not mean one has less status, privilege, or responsibility. We are all members of one body, the church, and Christ is our head.

## Closing

Follow the suggestions in this section.

# Lesson 9

## Blessed!

### Before the Session

Obtain a supply of paper and pencils for the activity in "Getting Started."

### Getting Started

By this time the members of your group are no doubt well acquainted with each other. As they gather, ask each one to list on a piece of paper one or more offices they have held or are presently holding in the congregation or one or more functions that they have carried out that are of benefit to the church.

This may require some thought since most people usually think only of board memberships or congregational offices. Choir, Sunday-school teaching, participation in evangelism activities, keeping the building and property in good repair, and visiting the sick are some of the functions that might be listed. Urge everyone to be honest, but ask each participant to try to come up with at least one item.

After the group has gathered, lead participants in a prayer asking once again for the Holy Spirit's presence, guidance, and blessing during the session. Thank God for the power to express the unity that is ours in Christ in relationship with each other and with the whole church.

# The Class Session

Have a volunteer read "Theme Verse" and "Goal" for this session. Then read or have a volunteer read "What's Going On Here?"

## Searching the Scriptures

After reading **Eph. 4:7–16** ask participants to give you the papers on which they listed the ways in which their talents have been used for the church. Share some or all of these with the class. This should result in recognition by participants that all have talents that can be used for the church.

Continue by having a volunteer read the introductory paragraphs in this section.

1–2. Have participants make a list of God's gifts listed by Paul in the verses from Ephesians, Corinthians, and Romans referred to in these two questions.

3. Answers will vary. Have participants list as many gifts as they can that have been given to members of your congregation and to members of the church at large. The riches of God's gifts to His church should be obvious. Each one is a precious gift from God.

4. Gifts from the Holy Spirit are given to people who function in special leadership capacities in the church. The *apostle* is sent out with the authority of God to carry the message of God; a *prophet* is one who speaks for God, bringing a specific message from God to people usually in a specific situation; the *evangelist* is usually thought of as one who is especially adept at sharing the Gospel with unbelievers.

Scripture, of course, speaks of many other leaders in the church. Assistants are provided for the apostles to deal with the administration of food to the needy **(Acts 6)**. The church has bishops, deacons, deaconesses, and elders. Today we have ministers of youth, ministers of music, directors of Christian education, who work under the authority and guidance of the pastor. Each is gifted by God to be a gift to Christ's church. Consequently, the congregation should recognize its leaders as gifts of God while the leaders should be humbly thankful that God has chosen them to serve in their various capacities. There is no ground for pride or boasting here either, or for lording it over other members of the church.

5. Conclude this section by having participants try to differentiate the functions of those people in your congregation they have listed previously. Answers will vary.

## The Word for Us

Work through this section by having participants read the paragraphs and discuss the questions in the order in which they are presented.

1–2. Answers will vary.

3. God always gives His gifts for a purpose. These Spirit-given gifts are given "to prepare God's people for works of service, so that the body of Christ may be built up" **(Eph. 4:12)**. Leaders are to use their gifts to serve, not be served. Neither are they to do all of the work of education, witness, worship, etc. They are to train the members of the church to use their gifts to serve Him.

4. A further function of leaders is edification, building up the body of Christ. This can only be accomplished through the Word and the Sacraments, through which the Holy Spirit works to enlarge the membership of the church and to strengthen the faith of its members. These should be the means employed by church leaders to build up the body of Christ whether on a congregational, denominational, or worldwide level.

5. All of the gifts and functions that God gives are to be directed toward goals, in particular the three enumerated in this section of Ephesians. The first goal is that of "unity in the faith and in the knowledge of the Son of God" **(Eph. 4:13)**. These two ideas are closely related, since all false teaching contains a nonbiblical understanding of the person and work of Christ.

For example, if He is not seen as the Son of God, He is considered to be, if anything, merely a great teacher. If He is not seen as the Redeemer, there is no recognition of sin and the need for forgiveness. False understandings in areas such as these hinder or destroy the unity of faith and its outward manifestation.

6. Christian maturity expresses itself in our attitude toward life and its events. It involves the relationship of our Christian faith to all of life. It includes actions that are consistent with Christian beliefs and confessions.

Since sin remains in the world and in us, perfect maturity as in our Savior will not be achieved this side of heaven. Even the great apostle Paul could not achieve it, as he points out in **Phil. 3:10–14** and **Rom. 7:13–25.**

7–8. Read and discuss these questions. Answers may vary. We are to speak the truth in love. We need to identify false teaching and living and reject it.

At the same time speaking the truth in love also includes a deep concern for those who hold false views. This is important to remember in relation to the brother or sister in the faith who has doubts or is uncertain. The task of the Christian brother or sister in such a case is not to condemn but to strengthen in the truth. This has clear and important implications for our life together in the church today.

## Closing

Follow the suggestion in this section.

# Lesson 10

## Committed!

## Before the Session

If you choose to follow the "coat" suggestion in "Getting Started," set aside a coat to wear. Make paper and pencils available also.

## Getting Started

Give each class member a blank slip of paper and ask them to list an event that occurred during the week in which a decision had to be made that involved their Christian faith. Ask them to list only an event that they will be willing to share with the class later in this session.

If you feel comfortable doing so, you might wear an old, worn, or torn coat or other item of clothing that you can easily exchange later in the session for the item you would ordinarily wear.

After all have gathered, sing or speak together the words of "Renew Me, O Eternal Light." This hymn will direct the class toward the purpose of this session.

## The Class Session

Ask for a volunteer to read "Theme Verses," "Goal," and "What's Going On Here?" Lead a brief discussion of the passages from Matthew, Luke, and Revelation. Then move on to the next section.

## Searching the Scriptures

Allow the class a few minutes to read **Eph. 4:17–5:20.**

If you have chosen to wear the item of old clothing suggested in "Getting Started," make a reference to this as symbolizing the "old nature"; then put on your "new" clothing as a symbol of the change described by Paul in **Eph. 4:22–24.**

1. Individual answers may vary. Paul makes it clear that *every* area of our everyday life is affected by Christ's commitment to us and our commitment to Christ.

2. Answers will vary. Perhaps he might write "no longer live as Madison Avenue does" or "… as Hollywood does." Yet one does not need to point fingers at institutions to understand what Paul means. We are not to live as the world does. **Vv. 18–19** describe our present day as well as the time of Paul. Whether 1st-century Asia Minor or 20th-century North America, human beings by nature are corrupt and "darkened in their understanding and separated from the life of God."

It is certainly possible, if not probable, that many of the problems that plague society today are related to the non-Christian goals of many people. Acting with these goals in mind, people attempt to find satisfaction in alcohol, drugs, sinful sexual relationships, material things, etc. The acceptance of these goals is a reflection of what people consider to be important.

3. St. Paul lists a number of practices that are not compatible with Christian faith. Among them are callousness or insensitivity to what is right and good, greed, covetousness, lying, theft, and unclean speech. Perhaps the class will discover others as they scan this section of Scripture again. Certainly, the list is not intended to be exhaustive but only includes those things that are most characteristic and obvious.

4. In this section of Ephesians, St. Paul does not only emphasize the negative. He emphasizes the positive aspects of the Christian life as well. This is important since many people are always thinking of Christian behavior as being opposed to something. This may happen either as they observe Christians or as they hear their witness. Sometimes it is a negative witness, emphasizing the evils of the "world" at the expense of the positive witness of the Gospel of forgiveness in Christ with its accompanying joy and recognition of opportunities for service. Paul stresses these opportunities and presents them. A list of them would include truthful speech, honest work, words that build people up, kindness, forgiveness, and thankfulness.

## The Word for Us

If class members are willing, have several share the event they listed at the beginning of this session. See "Getting Started." Allow for a brief discussion if the class so desires, but do not allow the discussion to wander from the focus of this lesson. After a few minutes guide participants back to this section of the study.

1. Unfortunately, even within the church, the truth is not always told. Truth is sometimes distorted by omitting certain facts, overemphasizing other facts, or presenting gossip in a way that implies fact. Because of our sinful nature, it is difficult to forgive and easy to become bitter and angry when we have been dealt with unfairly or untruthfully. Obedience to authority within the church is another example of an action that involves

love, forgiveness, and concern for each other rather than first of all for self. You can easily multiply the situations in which it is apparent that the old sinful nature must be put off and the new life in Christ that God has given us put on.

2. St. Paul's advice is blunt: "In your anger do not sin: Do not let the sun go down while you are still angry." Some anger is sinful; some is not. No anger is to outlive the day.

3. Our actions are reflections of the belief to which we are committed. They do not save us or put us into a right relationship with God. Only the grace of God can do that as the Holy Spirit works faith in our hearts. This is what Dr. Walther had in mind when he proposed his theses for discussion. If we teach that salvation is due to our actions of putting off and putting on, it is a rejection of the declaration that "by grace you have been saved, through faith—and this not from yourselves, it is the gift of God—not by works, so that no one can boast" (Eph. 2:8–9). Commitment always involves positive action, but positive action is always a *result* of faith.

## Closing

Since Paul advises that we should address "one another in psalms and hymns and spiritual songs, singing and making melody to the Lord with all your heart" (5:19 RSV), it would be appropriate to close this session with a song of prayer and praise such as "Blest the Children of Our God."

# Lesson 11
## Related!

## Before the Session

Prior to this session you might prepare a large poster with the outline of a church building on it. Divide the building into sections, and as class members arrive, have each one list the names of his or her family members who are fellow believers in one of the sections. Be sure to have enough sections marked off to provide space for all class members.

If you prefer, you can use an outline figure of a human body, with each family being a part of the body. Christ, of course, is the head. Whether you use the illustration of a church building or of a body, the purpose of this activity is to focus participants' attention on the idea that Christians have a more important bond than family ties with other believing members of their family.

## Getting Started

As your fellow students arrive, invite them to add their names and the names of their family members to the poster (see above). If any poster sections remain unfilled, these can be used to represent other families that are part of the church, either in your local congregation or elsewhere.

After everyone has gathered, lead a prayer. Thank God for having made us His children through faith in Christ. Ask for the Holy Spirit's guidance and direction to live as His children in all aspects of life and especially in your life together as families.

## The Class Session

Ask for a volunteer to read "Theme Verse" and "Goal." Ask for a second volunteer to read "What's Going On Here?"

You may wish to allow some time for comments about the changing nature of the family today, but keep this as brief as you can in order to allow sufficient time for today's Bible study.

## Searching the Scriptures

Continue by having participants read **Eph. 5:21–6:4** individually, making notes as they read. Allow a few minutes for participants to write down their thoughts about Paul's words.

### Be Subject …

Have participants read the introductory paragraphs in this section, then answer the three questions.

For participants to fully understand and appreciate the impact of Paul's words to husbands and wives, it is important that they have an understanding of what marriage was like at the time of Paul. In Paul's world there was simply no concept of equality in marriage. Although the husband had definite responsibilities toward his wife, these were the responsibilities of a superior in relation to an inferior, responsibilities much like those that an owner had toward his possessions.

1–2. Paul does not abolish the "traditional" relationship between husband and wife. Instead he introduces into that relationship a new and radical idea. Not only should the wife be subject to her husband, says Paul, but the husband should also be subject to his wife **(5:21)**. Each should live as though the other were the superior one in the relationship. And as husband

and wife live together in that kind of relationship, the old idea of a superior-inferior relationship will disappear.

3. The basis for this new relationship between husband and wife is "reverence for Christ" **(5:21)**. The Christian husband and wife should remember that they are in a relationship with one another not only as husband and wife but also as fellow members of the church, the body of Christ. "Out of reverence for Christ" a member of the church relates to another member as he or she would relate to Christ, for all are members of His body. Thus the Christian husband and wife are "subject to one another" (**5:21** RSV) not primarily because they are husband and wife but because they are fellow members of Christ's body, the church.

## For Parents and Children

Have participants read **Eph. 6:1–4** and discuss the two questions.

# The Word for Us

## Be Subject ... Today

Work through this section following the order in the lesson. Allow sufficient time for discussion by participants of the questions.

1–2. The relationship between husband and wife is not the same in every marriage today, nor does it need to be. Members of your class will no doubt have differing opinions about what the ideal relationship between marriage partners should be. For example, in the Smith marriage, Jan Smith may be better-gifted in finances and budgets and retirement and investment matters than Ted, her husband, and so the two of them agree that she should handle family finances. In the Jones family, the husband handles the budget. Why not? Mr. Jones is a CPA by trade. Mrs. Schultz is more outgoing in personality than Mr. Schultz. So he is not at all threatened when she takes the conversational lead in social settings. By contrast, Rita Klein just *loves* to hear Steve, her husband, talk. Differing personalities and talents make for differing patterns in marriage relationships. *Recognizing* these differences, and supporting and loving one another is one way in which husbands and wives can be "subject to one another out of reverence for Christ" (**5:21** RSV).

Emphasize the fact that as Christ is the head of the church, so too is the husband the head of the household. As Christ loved the church and gave Himself even to death for her, so should the husband love his wife with the same, self-sacrificing love. The wife responds to the husband as the church responds to Christ—with loving service motivated by his love.

3. The divine pattern for the relationship between a Christian husband and wife is the relationship between Christ and His church. Husbands are

to love their wives "as Christ loved the church" **(5:25)**. The word translated "love" that Paul uses here is *agapaō*, a self-giving kind of loving that always seeks the interest of the other rather than of self. Just as Christ put the interest of others above His own by living and dying for all people, so a Christian husband is to practice such self-sacrificing love in relation to his wife.

Husbands are also to love their wives "as their own bodies" because "he who loves his wife loves himself" **(5:28)**. The new relationship between husbands and wives is not only one of mutual subjection, but is also a relationship in which the two are one. Though each is a complete individual, in their union a new "being" is created in which neither can be separated from the other **(5:31)** and in which the attitude of the husband toward his wife reflects the attitude of that husband about himself.

And just as Christ is continually involved in loving activity to make and keep His church holy, so the Christian husband acts in love so that His bride may remain pure.

## For Parents and Children—Today

1. "In the Lord" emphasizes that obedience flows from the forgiving and loving relationship in which Christ has embraced the entire family.

2. To "honor" one's parents is to respect them because of their position of responsibility and authority, given them by God. A child may not *agree* with a parent's decision and still honor that parent—by respectfully sharing his or her own point of view, for example, rather than by ignoring, ridiculing, or refusing to obey the parent.

As children mature they need to be given more responsibility for making the decisions that affect their lives, but that does not give them the right to ignore the God-ordained human relationships that are present, and in this way fail to honor their parents.

3. Parents are more influential than anyone else in shaping the attitudes and personalities of their children. As **Col. 3:21** points out, constant parental criticism will result in child discouragement and may be the cause of failure or angry rebellion in a child. While wrong cannot be ignored, praise for success is much more helpful. If both parents and children can remember and remind each other that they are God's children because of the forgiveness that is theirs through faith in Christ, failures and faults of each can be dealt with more easily.

# In Retrospect

Follow the directions in this section of the lesson. Ask for volunteers to share their thoughts. If someone is reluctant to participate, do not insist that he or she do so.

## To Do This Week

Encourage class members to complete the activity prior to the next class session.

## Closing

As a conclusion for this session, refer participants to the poster of the church building (or body) with the names of their family members on it. Point out that all family members are related to one another also as members of the church, the body of Christ.

Close by singing or speaking the hymn listed in this section.

# Lesson 12
## Employed!

## Before the Session

In preparation for this lesson gather newspaper or magazine pictures that show people involved in various kinds of work. Display these pictures where they will be seen by class members as they gather for the session.

If you know the occupations of class members, try to choose pictures that show these occupations. Actual pictures of class members at work would generate even greater interest.

Here is another way to introduce today's Bible study: clip from a newspaper an account of one or more strikes that are presently in progress or that have recently occurred. Post these accounts around the room. Most of these accounts will list the points of disagreement between the groups involved. Many of the accounts will probably reflect bitterness or even hostile actions.

## Getting Started

Use one or both of the activities suggested above to introduce today's theme. As participants arrive, talk informally about how one's Christian faith can be related to one's work.

Begin the session with a prayer. Thank God for the tasks that are performed by people through which life is maintained, for those who work to provide food and shelter, education, transportation, medical help, etc. Try to incorporate in your prayer all the occupations represented in your class. Also ask for a spirit of appreciation for each other so that our society may grow and prosper in a peaceful way.

## The Class Session

Ask for a volunteer to read "Theme Verse" and "Goal." Ask for a second volunteer to read "What's Going On Here?" or read this section yourself.

## Searching the Scriptures

### Not As Slaves

Have a participant read the introductory paragraphs for this section. Then have participants answer the questions.

1–2. The world situation that Paul confronted was entirely different from that which we face. Even in Christian households, slavery was the accepted procedure. No doubt many Christian masters treated their slaves well, but others did not, and they did not make the connection between their membership in the body of Christ and the practice of slavery that degraded fellow human beings. Christian faith was one thing; the treatment of slaves was another.

While Christians were never urged to rid society of the practice of slavery, the writings and teachings of the apostles made it impossible for one group to treat the other as mere property. When he wrote his letter to Philemon, Paul was writing on behalf of Philemon's runaway slave, who had come in contact with Paul in prison. Through Paul's witness, Onesimus, the slave, had become a Christian. Paul was now returning him to his master with an accompanying letter. As Philemon read Paul's words, he could not possibly consider one who was to be viewed as a dear brother in the Lord as a thing. In this way—the brotherhood in Christ, fellow membership in His body—the whole concept of slavery was undermined. In a similar way, by stressing the Christian calling of both slave and master Paul undermines the practice of slavery with his words in **Eph. 6:5–9.**

### But As Servants of Christ

Read the introductory paragraph, then have participants either individually or in small groups work out their paraphrases of Paul's words. In paraphrasing, participants may simply substitute the word *employees* for *slaves* and *employers* for *masters*, or they may revise certain statements to make them more specifically applicable to our economic system today.

1. Two of the guiding principles from this section that apply to employees today:

a. *Do your work well, not primarily so your employer will be pleased but to please God.*

b. *Remember that your work provides opportunities for you to do good for others.*

Class members may also find other guiding principles for employees in this section.

Guiding principles for employers from this section include the following:

a. *Treat your employees as fellow human beings.*

b. *Be fair in your treatment of employees, because God shows no partiality toward anyone.*

Again, class members may discover other guiding principles.

2. **Matt. 25:40** provides the key: "Whatever you did for one of the least of these brothers of Mine, you did for Me." Even the most menial of tasks can be an expression of faith. The depersonalization and meaninglessness of many types of work today are difficult problems to cope with. St. Paul's words can help the worker to see the larger picture and understand that even the smallest task being performed has meaning as an integral part of providing needed goods and services. Paul's words can also help the worker to see his or her job as providing opportunities for interaction with others in ways that show Christian concern.

3–4. Answers may vary. A primary factor in our economic system that causes people to work as "men-pleasers" is that it is often necessary to do so in order to "get ahead"—to obtain a position of greater prestige or a higher-paying job. There is nothing wrong with doing your work well to achieve personal gain so long as this does not require sacrificing your Christian principles or achieving success at the expense of others.

5. Paul points out that there is no partiality with God in order to stress the fact that masters (employers) should treat their slaves (employees) fairly. God shows His impartiality by giving rain and sunshine to all **(Matt. 5:45)** and especially by opening to all people the way of redemption through faith in Christ **(Rom. 3:21–25)**.

6. In **Eph. 2:8–10,** Paul stresses God's impartiality in His plan of salvation by emphasizing that salvation is totally a gift of God. No one can boast or claim superiority over others.

## The Word for Us

This final activity in today's session provides an opportunity for participants to apply the Christian principles developed from Paul's words to a "real life" situation.

Divide the class into two groups. Designate one group as "labor" and the other as "management." Set up a specific strike situation either on the basis of the clippings you brought to class or on a hypothetical situation. Have the two groups debate the issues involved, playing their assigned roles. If time permits, after a period of time have participants reverse roles; i.e., have the group that was "management" become "labor" and vice versa.

Hopefully, the exercise will focus participants' attention both on the problems involved in living out one's Christian faith in the business world and also on how the guiding principle developed in this session from Paul's words can help to do this.

## Closing

Follow the suggestion in this section of the lesson. Conclude the session with the blessing from **1 Cor. 15:58** or from **Heb. 13:20–21.**

# Lesson 13
## Armed!

### Before the Session

If you choose to use "A Mighty Fortress Is Our God" as an opening hymn, have copies of the hymn for participants.

### Getting Started

Since this is the last session of the course, you may wish to discuss reactions to it with class members as they arrive. No doubt you will be interested in knowing whether they believe that the experience has been valuable and whether they believe it has helped them in understanding what the church is and what its task involves.

Perhaps class members will also wish to give suggestions for improvement of the course if it is taught in the future. This would also be a good time to refer to future plans for Bible study and to encourage participants to continue in the study of God's Word.

### The Class Session

Begin the session by singing or speaking "A Mighty Fortress Is Our God" and/or by reading **Psalm 46,** the psalm on which the hymn is based. Both the psalm and the hymn contain thoughts that are parallel to those found in the section of Ephesians that will be discussed in this session.

Continue by asking how many of the class can remember when the entire world has been at peace. There will probably be few, if any, who can remember such a period of any length.

Now ask for a volunteer to read "Theme Verse" and "Goal." Ask for a second volunteer to read "What's Going On Here?"

## Searching the Scriptures

Have the participants read **Eph. 6:10–20,** then answer the questions.

One of the most difficult things to face is an unknown enemy. For example, if someone is opposing a plan that you have, but you do not know who it is, you cannot confront that person. If someone is spreading a false rumor about you, it cannot be squelched if you do not know who is making the statements. Unfortunately, these things sometimes also occur in the church.

Whether any class member has had an experience like that or not, all Christians are involved in a battle against forces that are difficult to identify. St. Paul gives a description of them that characterizes them as superhuman, "not against flesh and blood" **(6:12).** These forces are present, but it is difficult to identify them.

1. As we view history we can begin to get an idea of the presence of demonic forces that appear in the activities of people and organizations and nations. There are incidents of murder and mayhem, of genocide, of the destruction of innocent people in war, with all of the hardships and suffering that accompany it. One of the greatest horrors of our present century was the systematic extermination of millions of people in Nazi gas chambers in World War II. There are many similar events that can be recalled. One in fact needs to look no further than the daily news.

St. Paul says we wrestle "against the principalities, against the powers, against the world rulers of this present darkness, against the spiritual hosts of wickedness in the heavenly places" **(6:12** RSV). This phrase may be a reference to the demonic forces that are active in world governments as they engage in these activities.

2. Even the organized church has been guilty of falling into Satan's traps. Using the scriptural passage "make them come in, so that my house will be full" **(Luke 14:23),** the church of the Middle Ages forced individuals and groups to accept Christianity. Torture chambers were used during the Inquisition to eliminate heresy and force people to confess the teachings of the church. The Thirty Years' War (1618–48) sent a pall of destruction over Europe. Protestants and Catholics slaughtered each other in the name of the Christian faith and turned large parts of Europe into a waste-

land in the process. Those same forces can be exerted in more subtle ways even today if the organized church uses its power to achieve similar goals.

Satan and his forces are not just a figment of the imagination. He and they are very real and active in the world today. The power that they wield is reflected in the astounding growth of interest in the occult and astrology and in groups of Satan worshipers who are serious in their beliefs. They should not be underestimated.

3. The activity of Satan and his forces is subtle and cunning. They are described as "the devil's schemes" **(6:11)**. These superhuman forces are clever, disguising themselves in various ways.

4. St. Paul describes Satan as one who "masquerades as an angel of light" **(2 Cor. 11:14)**. Evil is disguised as being good. The "lawless one" **(2 Thess. 2:9)**, usually identified as the Antichrist, comes by the "work of Satan," performing counterfeit miracles and other astounding feats in order to convince others of power and secure their allegiance.

If we are honest with ourselves, we can recognize those forces in our own lives as we seek to rationalize evil actions by trying to justify them on the basis of the good we seek to accomplish. This, too, is something that can happen in the organized church. We can never forget that the church consists of people who are both justified and sinning—sinner and saint. Members of the church are not perfect; they are forgiven.

## Put on the Equipment

1. It does little good to be aware of or even to identify the enemy if one is not prepared to fight. That is why St. Paul twice in this section urges Christians to put on "the whole armor of God." Since the forces that oppose the Christian are superhuman, they cannot be overcome by human abilities. Protection and victory can only be achieved through the armor that God provides. He provides much and, since Satan uses all the weapons in his arsenal, it would be foolish not to use all that is available to oppose him. The power of Almighty God is available in His Word and Sacraments for the Christian.

You might refer here to Jesus' use of Scripture when tempted by Satan. He defeated him with the words "It is written." See **Matt. 4:1–11.**

2. Paul lists the armor of the Christian as being the belt of truth, the breastplate of righteousness, the sandals of the gospel of peace, the shield of faith, the helmet of salvation, and the sword of the Spirit, "which is the word of God." Altogether the "armor of God" provides everything that a Christian needs. A Christian gains this armor through Baptism, when he or she is united with Christ. To put on Christ involves receiving His power and the protection that He has to offer as the Holy Spirit strengthens faith

through Word and Sacrament.

3. The shield of faith protects a Christian against the assaults of Satan. Its opposite is doubt, which can destroy the spiritual life. Doubt was the source of humanity's fall into sin in the Garden of Eden. Doubt caused Israel to be condemned to a 40-year wandering in the wilderness; it caused Peter to sink as he walked across the water to Christ. There are other examples of this in Scripture also. Perhaps members of the class can list some of them. Among them could be the cause of Peter's denial, the fear of the disciples during the storm on the Sea of Galilee, and Thomas' week of agitation when he doubted that Christ had risen.

Doubt about the power of Christ and His forgiveness produces the same results today. That is why we pray in the Lord's Prayer, "Lead us not into temptation."

4. In urging his readers to take the helmet of salvation Paul is reminding them that salvation is already theirs. Salvation has all three aspects: past, present, and future. It was secured by Christ through His life, death, and resurrection. It belongs to the Christian by faith. It will be fully realized on Judgment Day.

5. To know that salvation is guaranteed, as was pointed out in an earlier section of the letter, enables one to live confidently. There is absolute certainty that Satan with his temptations can be overcome in his daily attacks. That certainty is there as the Spirit works through the Word of God to strengthen the faith of believers.

6. Note once again Christ's use of the Word in His fight against temptation (**Matt. 4:1–11**). The Word should be used in every form, including the Word that is spoken by fellow Christians, fellow soldiers in the battle against the devil.

## The Word for Us

The battle is a never-ending one in this life. There is never room for complacency. We are not to be overconfident, lest we lose the war even though we might win some of the battles against Satan. Satan has already been defeated by Christ. The victory is only ours by faith in Christ, faith to the end.

1–2. Since faith is a gift of the Holy Spirit, we need to pray that He will keep us in that faith through the power of the Word of God. That should be an unceasing prayer, and it will be as we live each moment of our lives conscious of our dependence on the grace of God in Christ. That is praying without ceasing. That can be done at all times and in all circumstances and will in no way conflict with the tasks that confront us as we earn our daily bread.

Each one of us needs that prayer on the part of others, just as others need our prayers for them. We are bound to one another in the body of Christ by the Holy Spirit. Together as the body of Christ we can conquer in His power and by His grace.

## Closing

A fitting conclusion for this session and for the entire study is the singing of the hymn "Onward, Christian Soldiers." If there is time, prior to the singing of the hymn, you could discuss any questions that still remain unanswered and that the group would like to consider at this time.

If time does not permit this, perhaps there would be a few moments after the class to discuss these questions, or another time might be arranged for this purpose.